Water

from the big bang to the bottle

Assouline Publishing
601 West 26th Street, New York, NY 10001
www.assouline.com

First published in French by Éditions Assouline
Eau, sources de légende © 2000 Éditions Assouline
English translation by Christina Henry de Tessan
© 2000 Assouline Publishing

© Cover photos: Laziz Hamani
© Chapter on water cures: Fabienne Rousso
Proof-reading: Siôn Rees Williams

ISBN: 2 84323 209 0

Printed in France

MICHEL DOVAZ

Water

from the big bang to the bottle

Photography editing by Stéphanie Busuttil

ASSOULINE

Contents

Introduction

In most creation myths, water is the primordial element, pre-existing the creation of the world. It is from the aquatic mass that gods and demons, microbes and islands emerge; it is water that generates the other elements in the various cosmogonies and water as well swallows them up like the Great Flood.

In Genesis, "… the Spirit of God was moving over the surface of the waters". "All was water, vast waters that had no banks", say the Hindu texts for whom the Egg of the world is covered by these maternal Waters. From China, where water is the vagueness from which the earth is released, to Polynesia, where cosmic power resides at the bottom of the waters, the gestation of the Universe almost universally takes place in the aquatic element. These waters are not necessarily those of the sea. For two reasons: because not all peoples had access to the sea and because, although the sea is present in certain mythologies, it is fresh water that fertilizes the earth and allows mankind to reap its fruits. For desert peoples, rain is truly synonymous with life, a gift from God and a benediction. Summoned through prayer and supplication, in Africa especially, it is the subject of invocations and highly-ritualised, specific ceremonies. The Koran calls rain "blessed water"; "God created all living beings from water" (Koran, sura XXIV, 45).

Rivers are always present in sacred representations: whether they are those that flow to the sky like the four rivers that leave the Garden of Eden toward the four cardinal points, or the infernal rivers, rumbling under the earth like the Styx or the Acheron of the Greeks. On earth, they are compared to a current of life, with its fertility and renewal, but also its floods and destruction, like the Nile that the Egyptians revered like a god. The Greeks offered their sacrifices by drowning live horses and bulls. In ancient China during the spring equinox newly-weds had to cross a river, a fertility rite symbolizing the passage of the year and the new beginning of the seasons as well.

Mild, limpid, drinkable, water is the origin and the sap of life.

Gushing waters, fountains and springs also occupy a fundamental place in ancient cults. They are the orifices from which water—live, virginal, pure, endowed with divine purifying and regenerative powers—emerges. As we shall see, hot mineral springs discovered very early on were considered to be divine and miraculous. And the myth of eternal youth—is it not linked to the Fountain of Youth? Nordic peoples and the Celts peopled their springs, fountains and rivers with fairies and genies in their countless legends. The relics of these cults remain very alive to this day, notably in Brittany.

Whether polytheistic or monotheistic, all religions grant fresh water a role that is not only vital and fertilizing, but purifying and regenerative as well.

Traditional Jewish proverbs, like those in the Chinese tradition, often compare water to wisdom… "In the heart of the sage, water resides", says one Hebrew proverb; Lao-Tseu teaches that, to him, water is the representation of supreme Virtue. In Germanic legends, revived in the Wagnerian operas, the water of knowledge emerges from the Mimir fountain. Christianity adopts and expands this symbolism; water becomes synonymous with spiritual life: "But whoever drinks of the water that I will give him shall never thirst; but the water that I will give him will become in him a well of water springing up to eternal life." (John IV, 14) And St. Anastasia specifies: "The Father being the spring, the Son is called the river, and we drink the Spirit." (*Ad Serapionem*, I, 19)

For the ancient Taoists, "the nature of water brings it to purity". Immersion in the water of the Ganges, the purifying river that flows from the hair of Shiva, is the way to regenerate the soul for Hindus. For the Jews, immersion in the water of the Mikvah, a sacred bath fed by natural springs, marks different ritual times. Early Christians practiced baptism by total immersion, for which sprinkling has now become the symbol. Water erases sin and the ritual immersion causes rebirth. The purifying role of water can be found in numerous liturgical rites, the most frequent being the action of crossing oneself upon entering a church after having dipped one's fingertips in holy water. The sprinkling of coffins or tombs erases mistakes and cleans away blemishes—exorcists proceed no differently. In Islam as well, ablution is essential; before praying, meticulous rules must be followed.

In his work *L'Eau et les Rêves* (*Water and Dreams*, 1941), Gaston Bachelard explains it thus: "It is because water has an intimate power that it can purify the intimate being, that it can restore the sinning soul to the whiteness of snow. He who is physically splashed is morally clean."

Vital, purifying and regenerative, this triple role attributed to fresh water since the world became the world has not diminished over the centuries. Of all terrestrial resources, water is the most precious, the regions that are deprived of it will forever remain barren, and water shortages seem to be the most threatening of ecological catastrophes. Since early Antiquity in all civilizations alike, legislation, restrictions and taboos have protected springs from desecration and pollution. In another form, in another language, ecological science understands today the validity of these sacred intuitions.

Mysterious Water

The birth of water

Before there was no before. Neither time, nor space nor energy. Fifteen billion years ago, the explosion of a "punctual mass" created the elementary particles—this was the Big Bang.

The Big Bang

In 1927, Belgian mathematician and astrophysicist Georges Lemaître proposed a theory: "The Primitive Atom Hypothesis". According to him, an explosion of concentrated matter was at the origin of the Universe, which has been expanding ever since. Mockingly, this theory whose pertinence is no longer contested, received the nickname the "Big Bang". The Universe enters into instant gaseous expansion. The temperature is unimaginably high, around 18 billion degrees F. From these nuclear fusions, a cosmic dust made up in great part of hydrogen nuclei and helium nuclei is released.

Millions of years pass, the temperature of the Universe decreases. These gaseous masses are not uniformly distributed. As soon as they reach a certain density, they are subjected to the attracting forces of gravity. This gravitational compression creates heat. As soon as the temperature reaches 18 million degrees F, thermonuclear fusion begins, and a star is born—thus the Sun is born.

We can describe the functioning of a star as the conversion of hydrogen into helium with a release of energy and a small loss of mass. The energetic gain is 26 million electronvolts per nucleus of helium produced. Stated otherwise, the nuclear fusion of one gram of hydrogen into one gram of helium releases 175,000 kWh of energy; in comparison, the chemical combustion of one gram of hydrogen releases 0.04 kWh of energy. At this stage, the Universe consists only of hydrogen and helium.

Several more billion years go by and the star that we saw born is aging. It is becoming a red giant. Its way of functioning changes. It has burned its hydrogen and produces helium. This very helium will enter into thermonuclear fusion. From this fusion, via the unstable beryllium, carbon nuclei are born. The universe is enriching itself. From now on, it is made up of hydrogen, helium, and carbon. The carbon fuses with a helium nucleus and gives birth to oxygen.

Hydrogen and oxygen: the atoms that make up the water molecule are now present. There is not yet any possibility of water in the stellar furnace, but in the periphery of these aging red stars, it is certain that water is forming.

The agony of our star follows the same process described above, but in more and more extreme physical conditions, with the volumetric mass and temperature both increasing. Heavier and heavier nuclei appear.

Stars are mortal as well. They die in two stages. First, the matter contracts unimaginably to attain a density of 100,000 billion, meaning that 10 in³ weighs 2,250 million pounds. This implosion is followed by an explosion, called the explosion of a supernova—a phenomenon that reaches an extraordinary scale and violence. This explosion creates a nebula, a planetary nebula. It is not as rare an event as you might think; in our galaxy, it occurs twice every century—astronomers have even been able to photograph it. Nuclei travel through Space and the heavier elements are synthetized. But most importantly, molecules form and local gravitational effects contribute to the agglomeration of meteorites and planets: the creation of the Earth bears witness to this.

Hydrogen and oxygen atoms are abundant. At a temperature of several thousand degrees Celsius, they unite all the more easily, necessarily, one might say, since they are subject to an electrostatic attraction and the molecules bond. This interstellar water can attach itself to solid matter, form comets and surround celestial bodies. Separated from the supernova, water turns into ice because the temperature is lower.

The vocabulary of matter

2,400 years ago, the Greek philosopher Democritus, asking himself whether matter was infinitely divisible, answered "no". He called the smallest indivisible unit an "atom". Today, the atom is the elementary constituent of matter, but we do not stop dividing and sub-dividing it. The atom consists of a nucleus around which orbit one or more negatively charged electrons. The nucleus itself is made up of nucleons: one or more positively charged protons and neutrons, whose charge is neutral (hence their name). The number of protons is always equal to the number of electrons. If one wishes to take it further, note that protons and neutrons are each made up of three quarks, of two different electrical charges (fractionals), either positively $+ 2/3$ (quark up) or negatively $- 1/3$ (quark down). Two positive and one negative quark constitute a proton (so, $+ 1$); two negative quarks and a positive quark give a neutron its neutrality. The number of neutrons in the different types of atomic nuclei characterises the isotope. For example, the most frequent isotope of oxygen is isotope 16; isotopes 17 and 18 also exist, but are rarer. The molecules are made up of groups formed by chemical or electric bonds of different or identical atoms. In the first case, one obtains a compound body, of which water is an example, one oxygen atom bonds with two hydrogen atoms: H_2O. In the second case, a simple body is formed, for example oxygen: O_2 (diatomic molecules). It is possible to break the bonds that hold atoms together. For example, the components of water—oxygen and hydrogen—can be separated by ultraviolet rays or electrolysis.

As has been already explained, water does not date back to the Big Bang, but is the belated product of successive nuclear fusions. It is presumptuous to give it a specific "birthday", but we can reasonably date its appearance: several billion years after the Big Bang.

Water in the Universe and on Earth

Before atomic physics, the birth of the 92 constituent elements of the Universe classed by Mendeleyev (1834-1907) could not be explained. For the same reason, the existence of compound bodies and therefore water, were no better understood.

The terrestrial atmosphere is humid: we estimate the volume of water in suspension in the atmosphere at 17,000 billion yd^3. Until recently, water seemed to be a terrestrial privilege. The technical means allowing us to discover water in our galaxy, or even within the solar system, were still lacking. It was difficult to explore Space with known optical processes. Everything has changed since the advent of satellite exploration, and particularly since the launch of the astronomic satellite ISO, put into orbit in 1995: programmed to research water in the Universe, it has located traces of it everywhere. The Orion nebula, for example, seems to be totally "humid". Closer to home, within the solar system, the Earth has lost its hydrous monopoly, the characteristic that earned it its nickname, "the blue planet". Earth, so rich in water (which covers 7/10 of its surface), seems almost dry if we compare it to Jupiter's satellite Europa; recently photographed from all angles, it turns out that this moon is covered with a 94-miles-thick crust of ice imprisoning a liquid ocean that might be up to 31 miles in depth.

On Earth, the total quantity of water has been estimated. The breakdown is as follows: 1,766 million billion yd^3 in the oceans, to which it is appropriate to add some 48 million billion yd^3 of subterranean and continental water, and as we have already mentioned, 17,000 billion yd^3 of water in the atmosphere.

It would obviously be tempting to deduce from these numbers that each inhabitant of the planet has at his or her disposal 262 million yd^3 of water, but everyone knows that it's only fresh water that interests human beings. The available volume decreases remarkably—to 8 million yd^3, to which can be added 131 million yd^3 of water made fresh by desalination, a very onerous and insufficient solution for 6 billion human beings. To be complete, we must add to this hydro-equation the water contained in the living cells of the entire plant and animal worlds inhabiting the surface, some 144 million yd^3.

Humans share "their" water with plants and animals. The plant world is a great consumer of water. Did you know that an average forest in France consumes, or evaporates, 39 to 52 yd^3 of water each day! With the exception of aquatic plants and animals, everything that lives on Earth depends on fresh water. In other words, rainwater, which follows four cycles. The first is the shortest: rainwater swells the rivers. The second follows a longer path because it is retained in natural and artificial lakes. The third cycle is longer still, from a few weeks to several decades: with difficulty the water seeps into the soil and faults to reappear in the form of springs or supplier the ground water, which is sometimes wrongly called fossilized. Finally, the fourth cycle, which takes thousands of years, water turns into snow, glaciers and polar or glacial icecaps.

On the planet, the cycle is closed. The quantity of water, in its states of vapor, ice and liquid, was determined hundreds of millions of years ago. However, the cycles can by modified, as well as the circulation and distribution of fresh water, either naturally or artificially. Finally, pollution affects water and diminishes the usable volume. Water, by necessity supranational, but whose uses are national, is therefore a source of conflict.

Water, source of life

No matter how far back you go, water is necessary for life. There is no longer any doubt that the first forms of life were aquatic. Two facts, each sufficient in itself, prove this: chronology and the physico-chemical conditions that existed at the origin of the Earth.

Chronology, because the precedence of marine life is so manifest that it numbers not in millions, but in billions of years. The most commonly-accepted stages are the following: we must allow close to a billion years for the Earth to cool down, the vapor to condense and the oceans to be born (linked to comets' water), and the "primordial soup" to compose itself. On Earth, plant life (plus a few microbes) developed a few million years before the animal kingdom would risk crossing the shallow gulf to the humid bank, and not by swimming upstream, as we might have thought, since fresh water would have broken the osmotic balance of the cells. This event took place in the Devonian era, around 370 million years ago.

Two comments are appropriate here: first, the logic of our notion of evolution would have it that the most highly-evolved marine animals leave the water for dry land. However, this is not the case: one of the fairly direct descendants of this bold group, the pararthropod that survives in the hot and humid soils of the southern hemisphere, is nothing more than a simple earthworm with embryonic legs. Secondly, those animals that abandoned their marine environment remain dependent on water. All those who did not manage to protect the water contained within their tissues, through membranes or shells, perished through dehydration and disappeared.

The physico-chemical conditions

Let us return to this primordial soup in which the building blocks of life are gathering.

The hypothesis of the energizing of the vital process following fortuitous but inevitable physico-chemical conditions estimated in terms of millions of years was formulated in 1924 by Oparin, a Russian scientist. For this biochemist, heat and water vapor issued from the primordial soup, associated with methane and struck by lightning, that is to say, the atmospheric conditions that existed close to 4 billion years ago, must give the light of day to these vital materials.

It was not until 1953 that American Stanley Miller had the apparently naive idea of recreating the primordial soup of 4 billion years ago in a container: hydrogen, methane, ammonia and water vapor, with electrical charges playing the role of the lightning.

What happened? In the container, amino acids (proteins) formed. What is more, in particular conditions, the alliance of two amino acids (peptide bonds) tend for reasons having to do with their electrical charges to gather into microspheres, which mutually attract each other and grow. When they become too big, phenomena linked to problems of surface tension cause them to divide and so on.

We know of plenty of other cases of spontaneous organization in nature, crystals for example, but the multiplication of amino acids responds to another chemical formula. These amino acids have been the dreams of biochemists since the theories established by Fred Hoyle in 1978 in his work *Lifecloud: The Origin of Life in the Universe*. The hypothesis upheld by the author takes into account the amino acids discovered in asteroids that could have cultured the primordial soup. The cosmic origin of these amino acids, which are not organisms, remains nonetheless controversial.

Regardless of their origin, the multiplication of amino acids, in the form of microspheres or other forms, cannot be likened to the birth of life in the sense that we generally define the word.

To this purely metabolic function, an information system that makes up what we call our genetic inheritance must be superimposed or integrated. In the primordial soup, various materials could have played this role. Without going here into the chemical details that led to ribonucleic acid, it is appropriate to make two points. First of all, time: hundreds of thousands of years were necessary for the metabolism and information support system to coincide. Secondly, efficiency: the superiority of this new organization over spontaneous stereotyped reproduction, as is the case of the microspheres. Another important consequence: the complexity of the information system does not have the duplicative "photographic" rigidity of microspheres; eventual alterations that become hereditary open the way for evolution.

Life is born in water and the evolutionary process gets underway. We use the word water here in the usual sense of the word. The water is not chemically pure (H_2O) but laden with mineral salts, trace elements etc. From the primordial soup to this day, whether water flows in a stream, from a faucet or from a bottle, it owes its power and virtues to the "natural additives" with which it is laden. If everything takes place in the primordial soup, it is because it is rich. It contains, for example, iron in solution from which the primitive bacteria that have perpetuated to this day nourish themselves (ferro-bacteria), as well as cousin bacteria that feed on other metals, all extracted from the same primordial soup: magnesium, manganese and copper.

Animals and plants will hide and protect themselves in water for 3 to 4 billion years, during which time only aquatic life will be possible. If a plant or any kind of being had tried to leave the water, it would not have survived the hostility of the environment: volcanic rocks, worn down by erosion, a mix of water vapor, nitrogen and a few traces of methane resistant to the ultra-violet rays create a rather strange atmosphere. No oxygen, so no ozone, and so no protection against ultra-violet radiation. Any exit from the protective aquatic cocoon was unquestionably destined to end in death by irradiation.

Certainly, this ultra-violet radiation generated a weak amount of oxygen through the decomposition of water. With hydrogen and oxygen separating, hydrogen, the lighter of the two, escapes, since it is not retained by gravitational forces; oxygen remains and bonds easily—this is oxidation. But this oxygen is rare and cannot constitute the atmosphere that we know today. It is in water that all of this will play out and that oxygen will be produced in great proportions. This took place 2 billion years ago, when the elementary forms of life had already been in existence for 2 billion years: a new exploitation of available energy appeared. No life exists without the consumption of energy. Up to that point, organisms drew their fuel from the primordial soup, essentially through filtration and the energy yield was poor. Nature devised a new strategy: exploit light. This is photosynthesis. In the shallow seas that were numerous at the time, light penetrated and the consequences of photosynthesis would drastically alter the planet and give it a large part of its current appearance. The famous blue algae, sometimes also green and yellow, often presented somewhat incorrectly as our ancestors, are the most ancient examples of this phenomenon.

Photosynthesis

For the first time on the planet, energy would accumulate in the form of yeast, or sugar. Photosynthesis assumes the presence of carbonic gas, undoubtedly of volcanic origin. Excess therefore became available, in the form of cellulose, and the availability of reserves brought a superiority and freedom to the organism that disposes of it.

For 1.5 billion years, organisms became more complex: jelly fish, worms, mollusks, etc., and finally a "cord" fish that is our direct ancestor. This cord that sustains its body prefigures our spinal column, to which our verticality owes everything, but this is another story altogether concerning terrestrial life and not aquatic.

Let us return one last time to the primordial soup because we cannot avoid three questions: why did life, which appeared in water and developed within it in different forms and prospered in it for 4 billion years, leave an environment that suited it and to which it owed everything? Why did it do so around 420 million years ago? Lastly, having left its aquatic environment successfully, why do plants still remain associated with it? All these questions are linked to one another. Everything happens as though life followed two paths: to disperse, giving itself the greatest chance of success; occupying the greatest area of terrain and the largest number of different environments, and also to find the best energy-giving yield. With regard to the second question, it is easy to reply that before 420 million years ago, the stratospheric protection of the ozone layer not having been formed, the terrestrial crust was unsuitable for welcoming any form of life, which would have burned immediately. But why did plants remain tied to this aquatic environment?

Plants were the first to risk leaving the water—that said, without actually leaving it altogether: their upper parts emerge on the coast and benefit from active photosynthesis. The excess of cellulose fortifies the cells and facilitates the development of stems. The roots can exploit the mineral-rich soil; the humid environment in which they find themselves enables them not to dry out, because they must fight against evaporation. Regulatory systems will subsequently assert themselves. At this time the vegetable world moves from salt water to fresh water. For reasons having to do with osmotic intra/extra-cellular pressure, the barrier between the two types of water had previously been insurmountable. This same osmotic pressure favors the circulation of water within the plant, this water that is so important for nourishing it and compensating for evaporation. This vegetation without leaves but endowed with needles—leaves will make their appearance later—developed for several million years, preparing the terrain for the arrival of fauna, which was still submerged at this point.

All the vegetation that nourishes itself through filtration obviously ignores the temptation of being earthbound, just like those animals whose adaptation to their aquatic environment was very advanced, along with those whose weight is admissible in water but who cannot adapt outside the liquid element due to their constraints.

The candidates for terrestrial assault were therefore small in size, capable of feeding themselves through a "mouth" and still fairly rudimentary on the evolutionary ladder.

A very primitive worm like the pararthropod, already mentioned, certainly represents the type of animal that left the primordial soup for dry land. It is not the only one to have gone toward dry land; others would have been the ancestors of insects; yet others would become crustaceans.

Once flora and fauna have abandoned the primordial soup, they would free themselves from it in no time. After having given them life, water sustains it; if water were to disappear, death would follow. To list the drastic changes stemming from this photo-chemical process is amazing:

- Oxygen spreads, the ozone layer is established, ultra-violet rays are filtered, the plant world can be born.
- Organic matter appears (carbon, biomass).

– Limestone spreads, islands form, sedimentary rocks, called detrital, constitute themselves. When the seas recede, these deposits will be over 110 yards thick.

– Carbon, diamonds, flint, clay, quartz and oil appear, either as a result of biomass or phenomena linked to the presence of oxygen.

– Finally, the conquest of the earth by the living world. Everything is due to photosynthesis whose algae started it all.

Dangerous water, useful water

We know the adage "still water run deep". Water, so innocent, can be brutal and murderous. Its power is extreme. The myth of Noah's Ark undoubtedly stems from the memory of a gigantic flood. Mankind maintains a strong relationship with water but the element ignores any measure of it. Rain, so long awaited and hoped for when it is needed, becomes formidable when it does not cease. Rivers overflow their banks, bridges are carried away, and villages submerged—at which point water becomes a calamity. When the Yellow River overflows, we count 100,000 dead. Water gives life but brings death as well.

If it devastates with indifference, it can help with nonchalance, because it is directly exploitable. The first water-mills turned a millstone. If we believe the Greek poet Antipatros of Thessalonika, the first mills that assisted humans were to be found in Mesopotamia, about a century before our era. The Romans perfected them, but we must wait until the end of the year 1000 for water-mills to spread throughout Europe. The modern form of the mill is the turbine; it exploits water under pressure, flowing through barriers in forced canals.

The transfer of water and irrigation, undertaken millennia ago with the construction of aqueducts, the setting up of reservoirs, dams and canals, the control of water levels, and hydro-electric energy totally changed the terrestrial landscape.

Do we have to include erosion on the list of calamities?

Water has eroded the planet for billions of years. Its current appearance is the result of three causes: the movement of the tectonic plates (movement of continents, the appearance of mountain ranges), volcanism and erosion. Gorges and rocks are obvious signs but also the spreading of glaciers resulting from the distribution of eroded rocks and earth.

Erosion can have dramatic effects when the mined cliffs start avalanches and mudslides engulf everything in their path.

Thus water is never mastered; the best we can do is to learn to tame it and work with it.

Disease-laden water

If water, the primordial soup gave life, bacteriologically polluted water is responsible for illness, epidemics, and death. It then becomes the "soup of hell", a vast cultural medium of enemies of human beings. If we believe the World Health Organization (WHO), 50,000 people die every day from water-transmitted diseases.

For twenty years now, the word pollution is news. The term essentially refers to atmospheric and rain pollution: the air and water get dirtier and dirtier, since these two types of pollution are intricately linked. Polluted air pollutes the rain, as is the case with acid rain and the major zones of pollution are common to both elements.

However, whether it is water or air, the notion of pollution suffers from the lack of a definition. We generally pretend that pollution results from human activities. What then of natural pollution? Sulfuric volcanic gases, the methane produced by animals, stagnant water, water charged with sulfuric or hydrogen ammoniac after its close proximity to the rocks?

To limit ourselves to the pollution for which humans are responsible does not help in the effort to define or quantify it. The most common definition remains the following: "Degradation of a natural environment by industrial or household waste." Life pollutes, as soon as there is combustion, there is waste. Until recently, nature took care of the elimination of pollution, like the vultures who clean up in the countryside or the rats in the sewers. Bacteria took care of the transformation of biodegradable material. Although they continue to do so, their work has become inadequate because modern pollutants are so diverse.

The notion of polluted water is all the more difficult to define because chemically pure water (H_2O) does not exist on Earth. If water is always "impure", according to what criteria do we consider it polluted? Despite the imprecision of the formula, we will allow ourselves to define polluted water as that which affects or destroys the vital processes of the plant and animal worlds. Now we can try to characterize pollutants, but they are countless and new sources of pollution appear daily. This presents two problems: how to measure, and therefore quantify, a complex phenomenon resulting from multiple and independent causes, and how to clean water degraded by so many factors of toxicity?

Quantification of pollution

It is impossible to express a degree of water pollution by a unit or number. One series of tests allows us to identify and quantify the polluting agents, without however, allowing us to add them up as these agents have nothing in common. The first measurement concerns elementary pollution, that of used or "domestic", water. Everyone has noticed the natural purification of water in rivers—polluted as it leaves a city and clean again a few miles downstream. Intense microbial activity attacks the biodegradable matter and recycles the water. This bacterial action is conditioned by the presence of oxygen.

Agriculture is, as we know, an important source of pollution because fertilizer—generally surplus—finds its way into the rivers, ground water and springs. It is therefore important to decelerate and measure the quantity of nitrates, phosphates and potassium. Nitrates, which are very soluble, are the most dangerous and make the water unsuitable for consumption once they reach 50 mg/l. Certainly, agriculture does not have a monopoly on the discharge of nitrates and phosphates since domestic waste (cleaning agents with phosphates and products with ammonia) is responsible for around half. However, aside from a purely chemical analysis we must ask ourselves three questions: where, how much, and for how long does the pollution last?

– Where? In the countryside. It is the nitrates of agricultural origin that we find in the ground water and springs.

– How much? An average of 140 lb/acre of surplus nitrates.

– For how long? In this case, time does not intervene, as there is neither degradation, nor saturation—only accumulation.

Nitrates, like phosphates, have the particularity of not only polluting, but also of amplifying pollution. This phenomenon is called eutrophication: fertilizers function too well in areas where their action is harmful. The result is an overdevelopment of algae, which monopolize the oxygen, causing the biological death—by asphyxiation—of stretches of water and slow-flowing rivers by driving out all aquatic life. Another addition to agriculture's list of flaws: pesticides, theoretically made biodegradable a few years ago.

Industrial pollutants, heterogeneous by nature, are often difficult to identify and even more so to quantify because the polluting agents, heavy metals, organic poisons, solvents, detergents, hydrocarbons and their derivatives situate themselves at different levels in rivers, often in the form of micro-pollution. Nevertheless, they can have an intense effect locally and destroy the fauna or contaminate it quickly or slowly.

Numerous difficult and expensive tests are necessary to make water potable with appropriate treatment. The European Union is attempting to standardize usage norms in the various Member States. It is proposing over sixty tests, more than half of which concern micro-pollution. (Everything here is a question of scale because it would be easy to prove that mineral waters are "micro-polluted"—they actually draw their healing properties from this micro-pollution.)

We obviously cannot skip over bacterial pollution in silence, which has been the origin of sometimes fatal epidemics in the West in the past, and which still do so today in Africa in particular—amoebiasis is just one example.

Pathogenic micro-organisms are counted and subjected to the germicidal power of chlorine whose presence is not always discreet.

One last type of pollution must be addressed: the radioactive pollution of water. This can exist in close proximity to uranium mines, is very weak for physical reasons relative to the ore content and does not affect the organism. There is no radioactive pollution resulting from nuclear plants since they use heat exchangers and closed circuits. There remain accidents however: the rupture of a circuit or a Chernobyl. It is true that there were radioactive clouds, and therefore radioactive rain. It is true that certain plants, mushrooms among others, can accumulate and concentrate pluvial radioactivity. But it is also true that the radioactive pollution of water and air is the pollution that is easiest to locate and quantify. The case of radioactive pollution of seawater, created by the reprocessing plants of radioactive matter, is less clear and remains a controversial subject.

On the other hand, we speak of "thermal pollution" with regard to cooling water discharged by nuclear plants, which causes the water to heat up by 36 to 38 degrees F in the area of the discharge.

This summary of the principal sources of fresh water pollution reveals the complexity of the problem, without even having entered into the details of the cost of these continual tests, or the delays that they involve (several days when bacteria intervene), or the impossibility of performing all the tests every day. In various countries, we have pictured inexpensive, easy and natural warning signals, consisting of having the water "tasted" by various species of minuscule creatures that live in it and survive. Regular counts allow us to detect any anomalies.

In the same vein, we measure the toxicity of used water by introducing daphnia, fresh water crustaceans less than 1/10 inch long—also called freshwater fleas—and counting their mortality rate. By proceeding with dilution, we can refine the measurement.

Convalescent water

Society uses three different methods to protect water: restricting the causes of pollution (for lack of eliminating them entirely), locally treating used water, and creating vast purification plants meant to provide domestic, or "consumable", water.

Regulation and scientific advances help restrict pollution. The prohibition of cleaning agents with phosphates in numerous countries is one example, the suppression of non-biodegradable pesticides is another. Eliminating pollution of agricultural origin altogether appears to be impossible, but limiting the use of fertilizer to what is strictly necessary is achievable, and has been achieved in certain countries that heavily tax any unjustified contributions.

Society is better equipped to fight against industrial pollution because it can demand manufacturers to build purifying plants, and in effect, specific pollutants are treated in specialized plants that are both simpler and more efficient.

The used water from metropolitan areas is treated in purification plants that all run on the same principle: retention of matter in suspension, biological purification with the addition of oxygen and multiplication of bacteria, and finally, the elimination of a few resistant chemical products, the infamous nitrates among others. We are seeking to simplify the work of these purification plants by making them more specialized. In the big cities, rainwater and used water are drained separately in order to treat them independently. The idea of adopting a double distribution system of "clean water" was considered—one for consumable water, the other for household use (washing, etc.), with the knowledge that humans only drink a small hundredth of the water that they use, which comes to approximately 250 l/day.

The modest savings, compounded by the high cost of putting such a system in place, and the risk of errors thwarted this seemingly appealing idea. The technique of partially recycling water developed in major urban centers in Japan, or even of totally recycling water as is being done successfully in satellites and inhabited orbital stations, seems more realistic.

These extreme solutions assume two preconditions: that water is rare and/or that the price is prohibitive. Which is it?

Rare water

69,000 miles³ of water falls on the continental areas in the form of precipitation every year (240,000 miles³ annually on the oceans). The demand for water in the year 2000 is up to 3,250 miles³ per year, or 5% of the total continental precipitation—with two thirds of this water devoted entirely to irrigation and agriculture.

With 95% of the "water in the sky" remaining unused, we are therefore far from lacking a ready source— an unfortunately misleading calculation because obviously neither the precipitation nor the use of water are uniformly distributed. Shortages result from this double distortion, making water, as it has been the case since the beginning of time, a source of conflict.

Irrigation today covers close to 495 million acres, a figure that increases by about 1% every year. Experts estimate that the percentage itself is going to increase for reasons relating to demographic pressure (from 2 to 2.5%), which will further aggravate problems and create new difficult situations.

The diverting of rivers, as in Russia, and the deforestation of the Amazon and of Africa—a few examples among others—bring climactic changes, and therefore changes in the rain cycles, whose repercussions are felt far beyond the countries concerned. And since most countries are linked by waterways, the diverting or pollution of a river upstream inevitably has repercussions in a country further downstream. The Netherlands for example is dependent on the Rhine and the Meuse for 80% of its water resources. In Europe, bilateral relations and the Commission are both able to settle potential disputes—all the easier because Europe is rich in water. (Only three European countries dispose of less than 3,270 yd³ per inhabitant per year—the United Kingdom, Germany, and Belgium—but even their situation is not cause for concern.) However, this is not the case for regions that are poor in water, such as the Middle Eastern countries, which must share and distribute from minimal supplies of water.

Water, more than any other resource, goes beyond national interests, but in most cases, countries object to a reasonable and long-term plan to manage it properly. Discreet international conferences broach the subject timidly, which is of little interest to politicians since ecological problems do not have immediate repercussions and are considered non-events in the news.

Miraculous waters

It is impossible to attach a date to the earliest water cures in the literal sense of the term. From very early on, humans bathed in natural springs, and ancient medicine empirically identified and made use of the healing powers of certain springs that were thought to be intimately linked to divine forces.

From the beginning of their civilization, the Greeks built their temples close to hot springs. In fact, the Greek word thermos meaning "heat" is at the root of the word "thermal". These thermal baths are said to be "herculean", because according to mythology, Hephaïstos, god of fire and metal (Vulcan to the Romans), made a gift of the hot springs to Hercules. In the Odyssey, Ulysses is "delivered from exhaustion" from his shipwreck by the hot water that Circe draws from a fountain to give him a bath. In the fourth century B.C., Aristotle mentions the Oedepsos waters that appeared after an earthquake, that so many sick people came to take the waters that the authorities imposed a drinking tax. We know that in the second century B.C. both medical and religious cure centers, called *asclepiades* in reference to the god of medicine Asclepios and adopted by the Romans under the name Esculape, existed in Lesbos, Eubia, Kos and Epidaurus. Priests and hygienist doctors were associated with these organized centers. Several texts reveal engraved inscriptions on the temples' columns attesting to the cures for which Asclepios was thanked.

As early as the eighth century B.C., the Etruscans appointed civil servants, *acquilegi,* to identify, study and supervise springs. Sanctuaries and sumptuous buildings were constructed around these springs. Roman Italy also practiced water cures, and soon after conquering Greece, the Romans encouraged Greek doctors to continue to research and develop water cures, which would benefit from magnificent installations throughout the Roman Empire.

The Gallo-Roman period supplies us with the greatest quantity of ruins attesting to regular visits to springs, which the Gauls and especially the Arvernes in the Massif Central region of France recognized for their therapeutic benefits. Their practice of water cures, like that of the Greeks and Romans, is linked to the cult of tutelary divinities like Borvo, Celtic god of springs, whose name gave Bourbon—which we find in Bourdon-l'Archembault, Bourbon-Lancy, and La Bourboule—and like Divona, a healing goddess who gave her name to Divonne-les-Bains. On-site excavations have unearthed numerous votive statuettes representing sick parts of the body and water diviners.

The conquest of Gaul by the Romans systematized and expanded the identification and the use of mineral springs. The Romans founded most of the establishments actually in use today, including Royat, Vichy, Bagnères-de-Bogorre, Aix-en-Provence, Vittel, Plombières, Sain-Galmier, Néris, Uriage and many others, like Bath in England, Baden-Baden in Germany and Bade in Austria, which all have vestiges of the Roman presence. Secondary routes linked these spas to the main roads. The buildings were arranged according to the four stages of a bath, as defined by Gallien (circa 218-268), to which corresponded the four separate rooms: a cloakroom, lukewarm room, a room with a basin and a very hot pool, and a last room containing a very cold pool. The waters were used naturally hot or heated by a system of furnaces and pipes. The legendary splendor of the Roman baths has inspired spa architects over the course of the centuries. Porphyry, marble, and mosaics of all colors, alabaster, gold and silver faucets, columns and cupolas, frescoes and statues made these places splendid palaces devoted to well-being. Seneca (circa 60 B.C.-39 A.D.) commented: "We think ourselves miserable and maladjusted if, on the walls of these places where we bathe, we do not see shining forth pillars of marble from Alexandria inlaid with stone from Numidia (…), if the arch is not hidden under glass." Hot mineral springs became a subject of study and all the Roman doctors asked one another about the origins, composition and therapeutic qualities of these waters which were said to be medicinal, hot or cold, and proceeded to classify them. The use of the springs became more medical and the emperors sent their wounded troops and those exhausted by the incessant campaigns to them; mud baths, poultices and fumigation were commonly practiced, as well as absorption by drinking. In the first century A.D., Pliny actually denounced the abuse of absorption by this method: "I have seen people swollen from drinking so much and whose skin was so stretched that it covered their rings because they could no longer rid themselves of the quantity of water that they had swallowed." According to Herodotus (circa 484-425 B.C.), cures went on for twenty-one days. We do not know the nature of the medical supervision of the treatments, but in Dax, where the Emperor Augustus accompanied his sick daughter in the early Christian era, the name of a woman working as a thermal doctor, Æmilia Hilara, is mentioned in the texts. We also know that travelling doctors accompanied all "civilians" and that the Roman army did not travel without doctors and nurses.

With Rome well on the road to decadence, the therapeutic role of the baths (which rapidly turned into a mixed-bathing experience) died out when faced by competition from bathing for pleasure. The spas became nothing more than luxurious and morally lax places which accelerated the decline of the Empire. When the barbarians invaded Gaul, destroying and pillaging the thermal establishments on their way, the last emperors, converted to Christianity, simultaneously battled for the survival of the pagan rites and the debauchery to which thermal baths are compared to this day, and even went so far as to order the destruction of certain sites. In Gaul, St. Martin of Tours (316-397), great destroyer of hot springs, drove hordes of new Christians, who were just as bad as the barbarians, into degrading the spas and mutilating the votive and decorative statues in an effort to destroy all traces of the ancient cultures.

But owing to the survival of ancient beliefs, the therapeutic appeal of the waters was so great that the great and small of the medieval world returned to them quickly. The Church, which began by rejecting water cures as a practice equal to sorcery, progressively took control of them, understanding that this was the best way to eliminate all their pagan associations and obtain greater control over them. The lords on whose lands springs were to be found entrusted them to monks—notably the Benedictines—who founded their monasteries, priories and convents there, building chapels and churches, sometimes so close to the spring that they were built on piles, as in Barbotan. The miracles of the saints replaced those of the pagan deities; St. Agile resuscitated a drowned bather in Luxeuil, the daughter of King Clotaire II was cured of leprosy at Bagnols... Pepin the Short and Bertha *a gran pie* took the waters at Néris and their son Charlemagne, who liked to swim as much as bathe, established the capital of his empire at Aix-la-Chapelle. His soldiers, like those of Charles Martel, continued to heal their wounds in the beneficial waters, as did the crusaders afflicted with leprosy for whom leper-houses and special pools were built. The sulfurous waters like those of Luchon and Cauterets in the Pyrenees, had a healing effect on skin diseases; plague victims also tried to cure themselves there. Numerous pilgrims on their way to Compostela stopped to refresh themselves in the small Pyrenean spas that lined the road.

Starting in the twelfth century, despite the sorry state of the spas, the wars that made travelling dangerous, and the epidemics and plagues, furthered by the baths' promiscuity, spas were numerous throughout the French kingdom, as well as in Germany and Italy. They were regularly frequented, especially by residents in the vicinity, soldiers and pilgrims. The waters seemed to do wonders according to all those who went. Margaret of Navarre healed her rheumatism at Cauterets where she wrote part of the *Heptameron* in the company of her proteges Clément Marot and Calvin. She brought her daughter Jeanne d'Albret who was thought to be sterile and who became pregnant by Henry IV shortly after her cure. Priories and abbeys continued to colonize the springs, and in 1402, the Celestine priory was built in Vichy at the instigation of Louis II of Bourbon.

The therapeutic bath

Through the impetus of Italian research, the Renaissance and revival of Antiquity led to a slowing down in the reorganization and development of the springs due to the anathema of the Reform. Prudish and moralizing, the Reform caused a retreat from thermal practices, which would only later be defended by enlightened souls like Montaigne. At the time, the spas had extremely strict codes of conduct and all indecent behaviour was severly punished. In the thirteenth and fourteenth centuries, it is from Italy that medical studies were written on the way to take the waters (*Treatise of Poretta, De Balneis Puteolanis* by Pierre d'Eboli). Catherine de Medici and Henry III frequented Bourbon-Lancy, Rabelais and Montaigne the Pyrenees spas, as well as spas in Italy and Germany.

Henry IV (1553-1610) was the first in France to officially recognize the therapeutic qualities of thermal waters by creating the general Pyrenean kingdom's superintendancy of baths and fountains. He added to it an administration responsible for visiting them, logging their characteristics, recording them in treatises in order to reveal them and maintaining the buildings. In the seventeenth century, Nicolas Abraham de La Framboisière, Louis XIII's physician, studied various springs including those of Bourbon-L'Archambault, Plombières, Dax and Aix, in Germany, and recorded numerous observations and suggested uses in his work, *Gouvernement requis en l'usage des eaux minerales* (government required for the use of mineral waters). Even if the puritanical atmosphere condemned the use of thermal spas, as well as public and even private baths, the aristocracy and more enlightened souls continued to take the waters throughout Europe, even though it was still rather unclear where to go to heal what.

The ability to overcome infertility was attributed to several springs, among them Forges, Vals, Cauterets, and especially Luxeuil. Married to Louis XIII for eighteen years, Anne of Austria had still not provided France with an heir. This caused Charles Perrault to write in *Sleeping Beauty* (1697): "There once were a king and queen who were so upset not having any children, so upset that no one knew what to say. They went to all the waters in the world." Accompanied by Richelieu, the royal couple went to Forges in 1633 to try to treat the infertility of the queen. Five years later, the future Louis XIV was born. Numerous people, among them St. Vincent de Paul who suffered from malaria, visited the place. The small Norman spa was expanded and embellished for the occasion, experiencing the beginning of its fame—it was here that the king saw the first play by Corneille, a comedy entitled *Melite*.

People are quickly bored and the thermal spas suggested recreation and festivities. Musicians, comedians and dancers therefore followed the aristocracy to its destinations and a small number of authors created entertainment around the theme of water in which treatments, the sick and doctors were often mocked, like the one by François Colletet entitled *Les Divertissements de Forges* (*The Diversions at Forges*, 1663). It is thus that games rooms and entertainment halls began to see the light of day around the baths. In Germany for example, gambling rooms developed, foreshadowing the era of casinos that would later be associated with the spa towns.

Chemistry was still in its infancy. Colbert, who founded the *Academie royale des sciences de Paris* (The Royal Academy of Science in Paris) in 1660, put two chemists in charge of analyzing and studying mineral waters, followed by Louvois, who was interested in the waters' qualities in healing war wounds. Soon, the administration of the spas and supervision of the use of the waters were entrusted to attending physicians.

Starting in the beginning of the eighteenth century, the sponsorship of the court and the provincial nobility (who discovered the decay and dilapidation of the buildings during their treatments) allowed for the renovation of several spas such as Plombières, Vichy and Aix-les-Bains. Under the impetus of the attending physicians, new spas such as Barèges and Luchon were built.

The spirit of the Enlightenment and the infatuation with nature, followed by the improvement of the road system and coach service attracted philosophers, botanists, economists and agronomists to the spas; Diderot went to Bourbonne, Voltaire to Plombières, Rousseau to Enghien, Buffon to Contrexéville, (the latter protected by King Stanislaus who became the Duke of Lorraine). The English discovered the Alps and the Pyrenees. In 1772, the year in which chemist Lavoisier published a treatise on the difficulties posed by the analysis of mineral waters, Louis XV called a royal medical commission to be responsible for establishing a list and status report of all mineral water baths. France realized its delay when compared to the English spas, such as the very famous Bath, German spas like Baden and Italian spas like Montecatini.

The Société royale de médecine (Royal Society of Medicine) was founded in 1778, and as early as 1781 was entirely responsible for selecting the water intendants and controlling the quality and use of these waters; the exploitation of springs was subject to its authorization. The expansion and construction of numerous institutions were undertaken, notably at Amélie-les-Bains, Molitg, Mont-Dore and many small spas in order to replace the local buildings which were still made of wood and often rudimentary, particularly in the mountainous regions. New roads were built, especially in the Pyrenees, to facilitate access to the smaller spas like Eaux-Bonnes, Salies-de-Béarn, Cauterets, Bagnères-de-Bigorre, which soon replaced Forges as the fashionable place to go. Following classic norms, the architecture was functional and the galleries of arcades allowed people to stroll around pleasantly. Although with the exception of Forges and Bagnères, it was the foreign spas that attracted the most glittering international aristocracy—who came to be seen and entertain themselves more than for treatment—the French stations received the numerous wounded from the incessant wars of the eighteenth century.

The loveliest and most sparkling of the spa towns of the eighteenth century was unquestionably Bath, in England, where treatment followed an extremely precise ritual. As early as 1706, this city had a pump room and it was the first to create a magnificent collective layout from which other spas would take inspiration. *The Bath Journal* (from 1774) announced in its pages the arrival of notable people, who were also greeted by a special ringing of the abbey bells. Groups of musicians hired by the town council came to serenade them at sunrise or sunset. Then they received a visit from the physician who would prescribe the duration of their treatment. Games, strolling along the paved terraces, shopping in the boutiques, buying from the artisans (who had come here to ply their trade in great numbers), the long banquets and the twice-weekly balls all made Bath the place to go for holidays.

In France, the Revolution suspended the construction of great creations planned by the Old Regime, but, even if they had momentarily expelled the aristocracy, the abolition of privileges and nationalization of ecclesiastical and noble goods democratized the water cure industry. The various regimes that followed in rapid order in the first half of the politically chaotic nineteenth century did not prohibit the administrative continuity of the management of the water cure industry in France. The royal intendants were replaced by prefects and the would-be physicians of the Old Regime by medical inspectors who were entrusted, like their predecessors, with a simultaneously medical and administrative role. The State took back the responsibility of assisting the sick and destitute, until then undertaken in large part by the Church.

The stampede towards water

The very new nobility of the French Empire, mixing with the old aristocracy back from its forced emigration, found its way to the spa towns and an imperial decree in 1806 authorized them to organize gambling during the season. The numerous members of the Bonaparte family especially loved taking the waters, from Aix-les-Bains to Vichy, from Plombières to Barèges, reserved for the military, where the princes and the imperial marshals came to heal wounds inflicted during the Napoleonic campaigns and where Hortense de Beauharnais founded a hospital for the poor. Louis XVIII and his court followed, as well as those of Charles X and Louis-Philippe, whose wife Queen Amélie discovered Bains-sur-Tech, a small spa in the Pyrenees which would later take the name Amélie-les-Bains in her honor. The British had been very fond of the Pyrenees ever since Dr. Meigham wrote a work in 1742 singing the praises of the Barèges waters and the region's climate. The Russians also went there. These foreign newcomers began to have holiday chalets built around the springs whose architecture was reminiscent of the country houses of the various countries from which they came. It was the era of journeys dear to romantics, and the landscapes of mountains, lakes, forests and streams, both grandiose and melancholic. For the most part the natural settings of the many mineral springs, inspired their sensitivity. Victor Hugo, Alphonse de Lamartine and George Sand sang the praises of Cauterets, Aix-les-Bains and Saint-Sauveur, while the artists, Melling, Hardy and Nattes, filled their notebooks with drawings and watercolors, inspiring numerous other travelers in turn. Starting in 1830, the distribution of lithographs, like those of Gavarni, blending landscapes and elegant scenes and some of which illustrated the first tourist guides, further increased the public craze for mineral springs.

The Second Empire in France opened the way for water cures' high point during the *Belle Epoque*. Napoleon III loved the mineral spas and greatly contributed to their development. In his fourteen-year reign, the Emperor spent eleven seasons in different spa towns, notably Vichy, Royat, Saint-Sauveur and

Plombières. For her part, Eugénie de Montijo had been an enthusiast of cures since adolescence when her mother had taken her from Germany to the Pyrenees. Once empress, she often returned, had her son cured at Bagnères-de-Luchon, and in 1861, gave her name to the baths of Saint-Loubouer, known as Eugénie-les-Bains ever since.

Following the imperial couple, the court, international aristocracy and upper echelons of the bourgeoisie discovered and enjoyed the benefits of cures and the luxurious atmosphere of the spas. Napoleon III often received sovereigns and foreign ministers there and handled numerous international affairs in their discreet and relaxed atmosphere, to the point where columnists of the time referred to the emperor's "thermal diplomacy". But beyond the many anecdotes on the life and recreational activities of Napoleon III at the baths, the emperor legislated and accelerated the modernization of the spas, which he endowed with new equipment and new access routes by road and train. At Plombières, where the sumptuous *Thermes Napoleon* were built, he supervised the progress of the work himself. It was there that in July 1858 he met Cavour, the Italian minister of Foreign Affairs and decided to declare a war on Austria that would determine Italian unity. In the early twenties, in his book *The Guermantes Way*, Marcel Proust expressed this secret diplomacy in the following way: "A dialogue in which destiny would dictate the word War or Peace generally never took place in the advisors' cabinet but on the bench of a *Kungarten* where the minister and M. de Norpois both went to the mineral water fountains to drink small glasses of curative water from the spring. By a sort of tacit agreement, they met at the hour of the treatment and took the few steps of a stroll that, though benign in appearance, the two speakers knew to be as tragic as a mobilization order."

Napoleon III also modernized Saint-Sauveur and opened a railway line linking the small Pyrenean spa to Tarbes. But it is Vichy, after his first visit in 1861, that would long remain the great beneficiary of the emperor's generosity and which became the capital of French water cures. Between 1852 and 1870, the visits to Vichy multiplied threefold, transforming this small village into a big city, all built up in a few short years: a city hall, church, train station, theatre and casino, new roads and English-style parks, big hotels and luxury commerce all materialized. Napoleon III had the first casino ever built on French soil constructed and inaugurated in Vichy on July 2, 1865. In the spa town, the casino quickly became a central institution, the counterpart of the spring, around which free time away from the actual treatment was organized, as well as the idle time of family and friends who had accompanied the person being treated. The tourist brochures suggested that visitors subscribe to the casino, like the *Guide Philips* which in 1870 wrote: "It is clear that if you stay at Vichy for more than a week, you will have subscribed to the casino," not forgetting to add: "If you have not yet done so, hurry, as it is an absolute necessity." The overall cost of a treatment therefore included a price for the casino equal to that of a doctor. Note however that the casino was not yet, at least in France, a lounge devoted to gambling, but that it played the role of a reception and cultural recreation center. In the hall, dispatches from the newly-opened Havas agency were posted daily; in the reading room, in a family atmosphere, one could rest between trips to the baths and the refreshment room—because the person being treated got off to a very early start in the morning, around 4:45, for an hour-and-a-half-long bath. Newspapers, reviews and board games were available, the women making use of a private room with a piano if they wished to be alone. At 11 a.m., the first concert took place, performed on the terrace or under the bandstand in the park. In season, the casino maintained its own orchestra— chamber or symphonic depending on the size of the spa—and indeed often a lyrical or theatrical troupe; the most fashionable spa towns becoming, among other things, necessary stops on Parisian and international stars and great opera and operetta divas tours. Music was the social link at the spas, punctuating the treatments, and like the pool and casino, the bandstand was an integral part of the town; in the bigger ones, like Vichy, the concerts went on throughout the day—and at least twice a day in the more modest spas. Hotels and breweries also had orchestras that played at lunch, tea time and dinner. In addition, the casino gave balls, parties and gala events at least once a week. The more pleasures a spa offered, the more it was frequented by a wealthy clientele, more attracted by its status than by its treatments.

The fame of the spas that were in vogue stimulated visits to the more modest springs. Mayors and notable locals dreamed of making their small institution a little Spa or Vichy and soon to rival the bigger spas in medical equipment, hotels and recreation. The imperial impulse survived the emperor, and the return of the French Republic, the third by that name, did not stop the bankers' and industrial investments or the visits by crowned royalty: Queen Victoria, Leopold of Belgium, Victor Emmanuel II, and George I of Greece, regularly frequented Aix-les-Bains, while Vichy received the Shah of Persia. In season, the various rail companies added trains to their regular lines, which, like the Vichy-Express and the Luchon-Express, went from Paris directly to the spas.

Due to the prosperity of the era, the progress of science and techniques that improved the effects of water cure therapy, the extension of the railway system, and the significant growth of tourism, illustrated guides, and advertising in the form of superb posters, the rapid expansion of water cures during the nineteenth century caused regions which were difficult to reach to emerge from their isolation, and for the first time in history, reunited the elements of a tourist economy that would only continue to expand.

In the first years of the century, numerous new wells were sunk, leading to the creation of new spas like that of La Roche-Posay and numerous springs known by the Romans were re-discovered and renovated, such as Avene and Royat.

At the beginning of the twentieth century, there were approximately two hundred and ten active springs; more or less frequented according to their size, they received a total of more than three hundred thousand visitors annually. Technology made rapid advances and the collective baths in pools were replaced by individual baths, and especially by all kinds of internal and external showers and jets that made for the better utilisation of the water. Endowed with electricity, running water and heating systems, the first luxury hotels opened their doors in Vittel, Évian and Vichy. These hotels received the presidents of the French Republic and Council and all the intellectual and artistic elite congregated there each season, like Anna de Noailles and Marcel Proust at Evian. The metal structures of the machine pavilion of the Universal Exhibition found a new life in Vichy: they served as supports for the covered galleries where the lovely ladies strolled. Gabrielle Chanel, a young music-hall singer at the time, went to Vichy in 1906 to try to get herself hired. Opera and fantasy shows were all the rage and four variety show halls presented the best Parisian productions. Rejected, Chanel served water at the refreshment room of the big restaurant for a season.

Apart from a cosmopolitan, rich and prestigious clientele, the mineral cures attracted more modest visitors, come from Paris or the big provincial cities and often inhabitants of the region. Those from the professions in search of contacts, people of independent means and civil servants attracted by high society, those seeking a dowry or a good match, tired colonialists, social and bourgeois, all rubbed shoulders with one another—without mixing too much—around the refreshment areas and bandstands; a small world mocked by Labiche in several of his comedies and by Colette in *Claudine Goes Away*.

New sports took hold, like mountaineering and cycling recommended for those suffering from "gout, obesity or diabetes", and golf, brought over to France by the British. Tolerated more than authorized, except at the Vichy casino since 1898, gambling was regulated by a law in 1907 granting 15% of gross receipts to the State. But this closed world, turning in on itself narcissistically like a dizzying waltz, would not be able to withstand the assault of the Great War.

The democratization of water cures

The roaring twenties renewed ties with the water cure industry. Increasing numbers of wealthy foreigners set up their summer quarters in the big spa centers. Americans and Canadians who had often discovered France during the war now joined the Europeans and Russians. Uriage and Cambo quickly became fashionable Mistinguett and Maurice Chevalier, Colette and Lucien Guitry, Princess Bibesco and the Windsors, Edward VII of the United Kingdom and Alphonse XIII of Spain all met up there. Sports took on an increasingly important role, with tennis tournaments, regattas on the lakes, automobile and beauty competitions, and even the airplane at the Aero-Club of Vichy. People gambled more than ever at the casinos, whose number multiplied; orchestras played jazz and tango and the music-halls never emptied. In these high-society water cure centers, the number of vacationers far outnumbered those who came for treatment, who preferred the smaller and more affordable springs. Vichy was, at the time, more and better frequented than the French Riviera.

Although the international élite continued to stream to the spas, the water cure industry extended itself to the upper-middle and middle-classes: the trains became electric, the bus a very practical form of group transport and the social laws of the Popular Front, which introduced paid holidays in 1936, allowed hundreds of thousands of people to discover the joys and benefits of the springs. Leo Lagrange, a very active Secretary of State of Recreation and Sport, developed social tourism. Notably, he went to Luchon where he urged the water cure corporations to put in place new infrastructures that would be within the reach of working-class wallets. Family pensions, furnished homes, camp grounds, festivities and group sports developed rapidly, provoking the exodus of high society toward the Italian and Austrian spas, in particular, central-European, like those at Karlsbad and Marienbad, whose magnificent Art Nouveau architecture still bears witness to their splendor.

Social water cures

The law of September 24, 1919 had already created the Fédération thermale française (French federation of Thermalism) and granted communities endowed with springs the specific status of "hydromineral institutions"; in 1921, a list had been made of the spas having use of specific structures for receiving the numerous wounded and gas victims of the Great War. The creation of social security in 1945, the decrees of 1947 recognizing the therapeutic uses of mineral water and the January 5, 1950 circular by the Minister of Labor authorizing social security to cover the expenses of treatment, drastically altered the water cure industry. This takeover led on the one hand to a more rigorous medicalization of treatment, requiring the spas' to specifically define the therapeutic qualities based on each spring's properties and a radical change in clientele on the other.

The destiny of the water cure spas became linked to sometimes hesitant and contradictory social politics. The means were lacking to modernize the luxurious, but technically outdated, infrastructures and the sumptuous Art Deco luxury hotels that had been built during the Second Empire and the *Belle Epoque* closed or were renovated to accommodate more modest homes or two-star hotels. The fires were out and the touristic appeal of the spa towns diminished for a public whose tastes were evolving. Those that were still attracted by notions of chic spas now headed to the Italian sites, which were better able to reconcile social and touristic demands.

Relaxation water cures

Paradoxically, it is the taste for thalassatherapy, developed in France by Louison Bobet, that re-energized the water cure industry in the seventies and eighties. Some twenty years ago, a real jumpstart occurred based on the notion of getting back in shape, which is so dear to our era of overwork and continual stress. One after the other, the French spas began to modernize their equipment, renovate their installations and offer, parallel to the specific medical treatments, a concept of global care that incorporates balneotherapy, dietetics, relaxation and beauty care.

Water is no longer simply a curative treatment aimed at healing the sick; it also now treats the healthy whose bodies are simply over-worked, over- and badly-fed, with hair and skin damaged by pollution and cigarettes, the soul overburdened with worries... Hydromassages, bubble baths, multiple showers, mud and plant baths, wraps, steaming, draining, skin cleansing, exfoliation, masks of all kinds. The end of the twentieth century is rediscovering the relaxing and beautifying virtues of mineral spring water, its purifying, and therefore rejuvinating, effect on the skin, and now associates its benefits as much with those of plants and essential oils as with electricity and manual techniques. This enriching of the water cure industry by a whole range of complementary care, including muscular work and dietary consultations, is unfolding in a climate of luxurious cocooning aimed at relaxing and nourishing the soul. The wealthy clientele, consisting primarily of women, are heading back to the spas for short intensive treatments where the esthetician and the masseur are as important as the doctor. Avène, Vichy, Evian, La Roche-Posay, Molitg-les-Bains, Vittel, Luchon, Aix-les-Bains and others are staking their success on health and beauty, opening spaces and beauty centers, following the examples set by the United Kingdom, Germany and the United States who have more than two hundred spas that are progressively becoming very fashionable. Stars and billionaires have gone to the many hot springs that exist in California—Hot Springs, Rancho la Puerta, Escondido, and Calistoga (already known and used by Native Americans) among others—since the end of the forties to restore their peace of mind in fabulous complexes worthy of the most beautiful Hollywood sets. In France, it is Eugénie-les-Bains, taken over by Christine and Michel Guéraud, that offers the height of elegance in the water cure industry as it is understood by the twenty-first century, set as it is in a magical setting. The key words of these new sanctuaries for over-stressed executives are luxury, calm and sumptuousness. Taken care of completely, one loses track of time, despite the cost.

Water and the Law

The last twenty years have witnessed the rising popularity of bottled water over tap water. The opening of international markets has made it possible for us to buy spring water from around the world at our local supermarkets and nobody finds it strange to buy water in the same way as wine. Mineral water has now definitively entered Western homes.

Drinking waters are not all identical and do not all have the same characteristics; the law distinguishes between four categories:

— public water, brought by adduction, familiarly known as "tap water",
— bottled water, made drinkable by treatment,
   spring water,
— mineral or natural mineral water.

For the first three types of water, the law contents itself with requiring that they be bacteriologically and chemically clean enough to meet the standard of "drinkability". Mineral water is subjected to its own particular legislation.

Public water

Water "destined for human consumption" in Europe, according to the legal expression, is governed by the directives of the European Union of July 15, 1980 and November 3, 1998, which require the respect and monitoring of some sixty criteria—as against a hundred in the United States.

From now until the end of the year 2003, the European directives will extend European Union control of water distribution as far as the domestic faucet, and no longer only as far as the buildings, as is presently the case in many of the Union countries. This will necessitate replacing the current lead pipes, especially since the quantity of admissible lead is going to be reduced by new regulations from 50 to 10 mg/l. New norms will further increase monitoring of arsenic, nickel, antimony and hydrocarbon levels.

Bottled water

This water, made drinkable by adequate treatment and which must mention such treatment on the label, interests countries that cannot be assured of regular distribution of potable water.

Industrial treatment improves the raw material: after filtration, the water is mineral-balanced by the addition of various mineral salts, calcium, sodium, magnesium and bicarbonates (200 mg/l).

Spring water

The "spring water" qualification is attributed only to subterranean water, harnessed after drilling and put directly into bottles without any previous treatment. The separation and removal of iron and manganese that might make the water cloudy are not considered "treatment". What is more, it is legal to remove the carbonic gas and re-inject it to obtain a still or sparkling water.

In Europe, the bottling must take place on site, but this is not mandatory in the United States.

The physico-chemical composition of water may vary but the concentration of mineral salts cannot exceed the following specifications (in mg/l):

Magnesium: 50 – Potassium: 12 – Sodium: 150 – Chloride: 250
Sulfates: 250 – Nitrates: 50 – Fluor: 1.5

Its pH (measurement of acidity) can fluctuate between 6.5 and 9 and its total mineral content must not exceed 1,500 mg/l.

Although the name of the spring must appear on the label, its composition is optional; the law prohibits advertising the potential medicinal virtues of the water but allows information regarding its use in the preparation of food for infants. The wording "mountain spring water" can only be applied to springs harnessed above a certain elevation.

Natural mineral water

Like spring water, natural mineral waters are harnessed subterranean waters, not treated, and bottled on site. They are nevertheless subject to different regulations:
– Their composition must not vary, regardless of external conditions, from the output or the temperature of emergence.
– Their particular "favorable to health" qualities must be recognized by a medical authority—in France, by the *Académie de médecine*.
– Since the water's composition is stable, some of their dominant characteristics may be mentioned (see the different types of water below).
– The general standards of potability do not apply to them since, in being given the right to exploit them, the medical authority is the guarantor.
– The risks of peripheral pollution must be monitored.

– The water's composition has to appear on the label. However, the regulation is less clear when it comes to whether to prohibit or allow mention of its curative properties: while it is not permissible to mention "properties of prevention, treatment or cure of a human illness", it is legal to maintain that such a water is laxative, diuretic, or stimulates digestion.

Mineralization

Mineral waters are full of mineral salts and rich in trace elements. They distinguish themselves from spring waters by the immutability of their composition, due to the conditions of their creation.

Subterranean water behaves like surface water and creates paths following slopes and cracks underground.

We distinguish "ground water" from the deep layers corresponding to "confined" water. Ground water is supplied by the permeability of the layer above it, while the deep waters are hemmed in between two impermeable layers.

These deep waters follow the flow in the karstic reliefs (eroded or dissolved limestone) or infiltrate themselves through porous layers and flow as far as a watertight structure that is often carved up with cracks. Gases, most often carbonic gas, follow these cracks in the opposite direction and push the water toward the surface. In other cases, these layers of water held between two impermeable layers are subjected to pressure, which explains the force of the drillings and artesian wells.

Each mineral water spring is an individual case and there are no generalizations that can be made apart from the three following observations:
– Subterranean waters circulate—they are never stagnant, even within the layers.
– The circulation is always slow. Several years, and often decades, pass between the disappearance of the water into the ground and its emergence.
– Regardless of the geological characteristics (granite, flint, sand and alluvial deposits from all ages, volcanic ash, glacial moraines etc.) and regardless of the hydromineral pool, these long circuits always play the same role of an immense natural filter.
This slow circulation and the great solvent power of water explain its mineralization. The invariability of its path and the diversity of its geological composition create the originality of each mineral water. Faults that are close to one another but without any links can be at the origin of very different mineral waters despite the proximity of where they emerge. These differences extend to the temperature of the waters which, even in the same hydromineral pool, can vary by up to fifty degrees. The same reasons explain the presence or absence of gas.

Types of mineral water

All waters contain minerals. They "load" themselves up when they flow on or under the ground; we can therefore maintain that they express one or more soils. Mineral water emerges at specific places, whether it is a spring or a faucet. The law classes waters as a function of their degree of mineralization. There is no connection between the mineral content and the quality or efficiency of the water. It is simply that they are different, and some have specific uses. Four levels of mineral contents have been determined:

– Very poorly-mineralized water, with fewer than 50 mg/l of mineral salts.

– Poorly-mineralized water, with fewer than 500 mg/l of mineral salts. In the United States, a recent decision (1995) of the Federal Food and Drug Administration separates those that do not contain at least 250 mg/l of mineral salts from the mineral water category.

– Moderately-mineralized water, with not more than 1,500 mg/l of mineral salts. This threshold is also the one chosen for tap water.

– Water rich in mineral salts, with more than 1,500 mg/l; in reality, up to nearly 10,000 mg/l.

However, this division does not give us any information on the immense diversity of compositions. More than twenty trace elements and principal mineral salts combine in a countless range of proportions. We might as well say that the number of different waters is limitless. They are therefore classified in function of the three dominant components of their composition, which are themselves linked to various sub-dominants.

– *Sulfur dominant:* these sulfurated waters are either high in sodium or calcium. They emerge hot, are primarily destined for water cures, and are rarely bottled.

– *Bicarbonate dominant:* a vast category that can be linked to calcium, sodium and magnesium, from which stem the following sub-categories: bicarbonated rich in calcium, bicarbonated rich in sodium, bicarbonated rich in sodium and magnesium, bicarbonated rich in calcium and magnesium, bicarbonated rich in calcium and sodium and bicarbonated rich in calcium, sodium and magnesium.

– *Sulfate dominant:* We distinguish between sulfated rich in calcium (without sodium) and the fairly common sulfated rich in calcium and magnesium, as opposed to sulfated rich in sodium and magnesium which are not bottled but are used in water cures.

– *Carbonated waters:* Some of the water types mentioned above can contain a high content of carbonic gas (more than 250 mg/l) and become sparkling. These are generally bicarbonated waters.

Man and water

The role and necessity of water for human life has long since been established. While it has been proved that humans can go without food for an incredibly long time (more than a year), they cannot survive more than five days without water.

Water makes up 65% of the human body, even more in children and more again in few months' old fetuses (close to 95%). Without water, the cells do not function. Without water, there is no blood, and in general, no functions at all. The brain itself is a sponge (85% water) and the regulation of body heat also requires water.

The forty liters of water contained within the body renews itself through external means (between 1 and 1.5 liters from drinking, 1 liter extracted from food) as well as by internal means, in the form of 0.5 liters of "metabolic water".

Whether rich or poor in minerals, water brings to the body what is necessary for it to function harmoniously, namely mineral salts and trace elements.

Mineral salts

The principal mineral salts are calcium, magnesium, sodium and potassium. (We must mention phosphates, but only for reference purposes because water does not contain any.)

Calcium: of primary importance, especially for the skeleton which contains about 1 kg of it, calcium also plays a role in intracellular exchanges and blood coagulation. Unfortunately, the assimilation of calcium is difficult and requires the assistance of phosphorus and Vitamin D. A balanced diet should provide the body with close to 1 gram of calcium daily.

To be authorized to carry the information "rich in calcium" on its label, a mineral water must contain a minimum of 150 mg/l of calcium.

Magnesium: It is found in blood at a level of about 20 mg/l; it facilitates the metabolism and contributes to general equilibrium, both physical and psychological. The body's daily requirement is 350 mg/l, but the assimilation of magnesium is only partial. Only a mineral water with a magnesium content greater than 150 mg/l can be called "rich in magnesium", but whether it is present only in traces or in greater quantities (up to 250 mg/l), magnesium always contributes to the composition of mineral water.

Sodium: It plays a role in the composition of blood (3.5 g/l), as well as a strong role in extra-cellular liquid. Due to the contributions of sodium chloride, more simply called table salt, it is rare for the organism to suffer from sodium deficiency. However, excess sodium presents a danger for people suffering from hypertension. Always present in mineral water, its content varies from 1 mg/l to close to 2 g/l. The term "rich in sodium" means that a mineral water's sodium content is greater than 200 mg/l.

Potassium: Blood contains more 2 g/l of it and its presence contributes to muscular contractions and therefore to the proper functioning of the heart. 99.9% of mineral waters contain potassium, in quantities ranging from 1 to 150 mg/l.

The Trace elements

Although based on their weight, they seem negligible, we know today that these trace elements are catalysts that play an important role in vital biochemical reactions.

We can count several dozen trace elements that are necessary to human equilibrium; they enter the body in the forms of vegetables, starches and grains. Mineral waters contain many of them, the primary ones being iodine, copper, silver, fluor, selenium, vanadium, silicon, iron (which appears only rarely in mineral water, partly because it is an unstable element, and partly because water often has the iron removed from it), manganese and zinc.

– *Copper:* It contributes to the assimilation of iron, enzymes and like magnesium, proper psychological functioning. The human body requires fewer than 5 mg/day. It rarely contributes to mineral water composition (a few mg/l).

– *Fluor:* Its role in the prevention of tooth decay is known. This is so little contested that the World Health Organization (WHO) recommends adding fluor to tap water. 2 to 4 mg of fluor each day is recommended, but too much can create problems.

– *Selenium:* It is considered to have anti-cancerous characteristics in small doses but carcinogenic effects in too great quantities. However, it is recognized as an anti-oxidant and could therefore prevent aging. The daily requirements of selenium are infinitesimal.

– *Vanadium:* It participates in enzymatic activity and seems to have an anti-cholesterol effect. The body requires only very limited quantities of vanadium.

– *Silicon:* It contributes to the assimilation of calcium, magnesium and phosphorus, and is useful for maintaining the elasticity of tissue and bones and for maintaining cardiovascular rhythm. The 40 mg that are required each day are rarely lacking.

– *Iron:* It is necessary for the blood (haemoglobin) and immunological defenses. The desirable dose is 10 mg/day. Water often has the iron removed from it. However, a few waters have 2 to 10 mg/l of it in their composition.

– *Manganese:* It helps blood, bones and the functioning of the thyroid. The body only requires 4 mg/day, generally achieved through a normal diet. Relatively unstable, it is, like iron, sometimes removed from water. A few mineral waters contain 2 to 3 mg/l.

– *Zinc:* It aids enzymatic reactions. The body requires some 15 mg/day. A few rare mineral waters contain up to 3.5 mg/l.

The flavor of water

Some believe that water has no taste, and that it should not have any or it is considered suspect, defective. Others, on the other hand, only drink this or that water because of its alkaline, salty, sparkling or bitter flavor. For these lovers of water, some restaurants complement their menu of dishes with a "water menu", following the example of a wine menu, and in most establishments, both still and sparkling water is available.

But we do not drink water the way we drink wine, the sampling techniques actually being very different, as much in form as in spirit. Wine tastings are comparative and the reference models numerous, while water tastings, in some ways, are done in context. Tasters acknowledge right away that there lacks a single reference, a central point that we are in the habit of calling "neutral" (an ambiguous word that we must be sure not to confuse with other, obviously derogatory, descriptions like "non-existent" or "without character"), which supposedly refer to distilled waters. However, the "neutral" quality of distilled water cannot truly be appreciated by humans since it is tasted through the mouth, a humid environment constantly filled with saliva (1 to 2 liters per day). Lacking acidity, calcium, bicarbonates, chloride and magnesium, distilled water is different from saliva: theoretically, it should have no flavor, but in fact, it is unpleasant and can therefore not be selected as a standard of reference. When tasters select a reference water, a "neutral water", the water's composition is close to that of saliva. Therefore, are we not allowed to conclude that each of us has our own reference water—our own saliva? The whole question lies in knowing whether saliva has a flavor, and if so, what it is.

As we know, wine tasters sometimes disagree about this or that wine. We attribute this to "subjectivity", or different tastes.

Water consumers also notice different flavors and we can guess that the individual composition of saliva is linked to this diversity of flavors. Although the composition of wine and water has been the subject of systematic chemical analyses, the physico-chemical interference between the person who is drinking and what is drunk remains to be established.

However that may be, the similarity is striking between the composition of saliva and the normal components of mineral water, which all contain bicarbonates, magnesium, chloride and calcium. These are also present in saliva even if the composition is more complex, for apart from mineral salts, alkaline, sulfo-cyanide of potassium etc. we also detect proteins and enzymes.

Water tasting may, at first glance, seem simple, indeed, simplistic or succinct. It is in fact extremely subtle.

Obviously, if we compare it to wine tasting, its vocabulary is limited and the sensations less varied, although infinitely delicate. For example, if a "neutral" mineral water is poor in minerals, the tasters may consider it to be "without notable flavors", it being understood that for a taster to say that a water is "without flavor" can very well mean that it has a "good flavor".

Water tasting, like that of wine, is subjected to visual, scent and taste tests.

The visual test: the visual examination of spring and mineral waters does not provide any information since the slow path of the water along the ground filters them. The turbidity of tap water is constantly supervised; those obtained through manofiltration never pose any problems.

The scent test: three situations can distinguished: sulfurous waters, rarely bottled; tap water, whose treatment phases include de-gassing which is, in theory, odorless until the dose of chlorine destined to prevent bacterial growth is added to it; and spring and mineral water, which are for the most part odorless. The tasters' vocabulary is sometimes strange when they express a metallic smell (iron, manganese, copper), a gunflint scent (an expression also used by wine experts), or an acidic fragrance; the "mineral" quality is reminiscent of the smell of humid chalk or soil, while the word "pharmaceutical", resulting undoubtedly from the presence of bicarbonates, reminds one of aspirin.

The taste test: the most important step takes place in the mouth. Since waters do not have a uniform flavor, the classic notions of balance and harmony intervene. Although the "aromatic" contributions are relatively few, their variable proportions contribute to the unique character of each water.

The four fundamental flavors depend on the composition of the water, but experience has proved that reading the analytic text about a water does not allow one to predict its flavor—which is equally true for wine—the blending among the components confounding any predictions.

Chloride and sulfates bring a salty touch, as do magnesium salts, with a bitter edge as well. Magnesium and sulfates support each other; magnesium sulfates are bitter. Alkaline flavors can be found in bicarbonated waters; calcium plays a flexible and moderating role.

The taster is also sensitive to the mechanical effects, the first obvious with regard to carbonated water working directly on the tongue and the oral mucous membranes, the other more discreet and rare effect produced by astringent water (a constricting effect). All the same, it is the impression of heaviness and stillness, as opposed to fluidity and lightness that remains for most consumers the most important characteristics, that some summarize in a succinct formula: "There are more thirst-quenching waters than others". With the exception of distilled water, which, entirely without minerals, belongs to the category of heavy and still waters, one cannot define an *ipso facto* water as being part of this category or the other! What one should not conclude is that there is a minimum threshold of mineralization any more than a ceiling (Saint-Yorre: 4.774 mg/l, Charrier: 37 mg/l). Here again, it is the group of components that creates the balance.

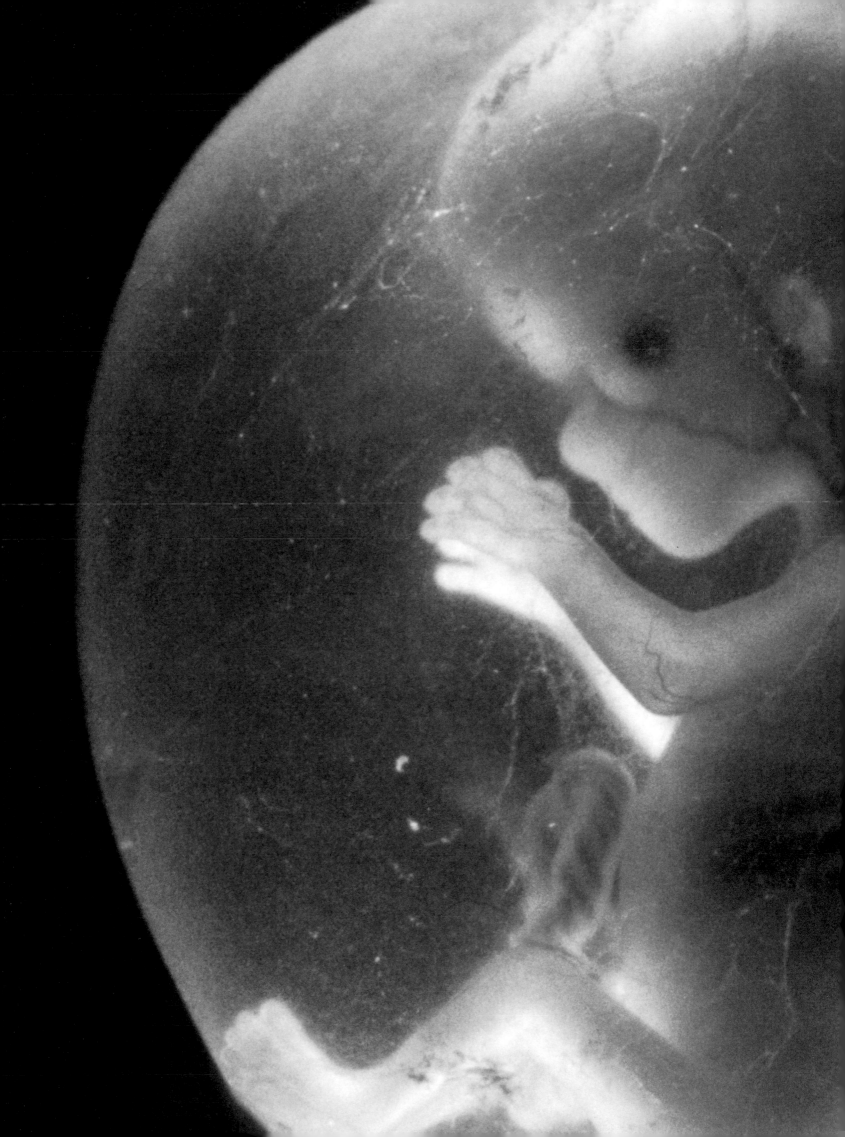

[4] Crystals, six-branch stars.

Above:

[12] Fire and water.

Facing page:

[13] Waimea Bay, on the island of Oahu, Hawaii, USA.

Following pages:

[14] Diver amidst a school of barracudas in Papua New Guinea.

[15] Roped party on the ridge of a glacier.

Glacial run-off adds 2,500 km³ of water to the oceans each year.

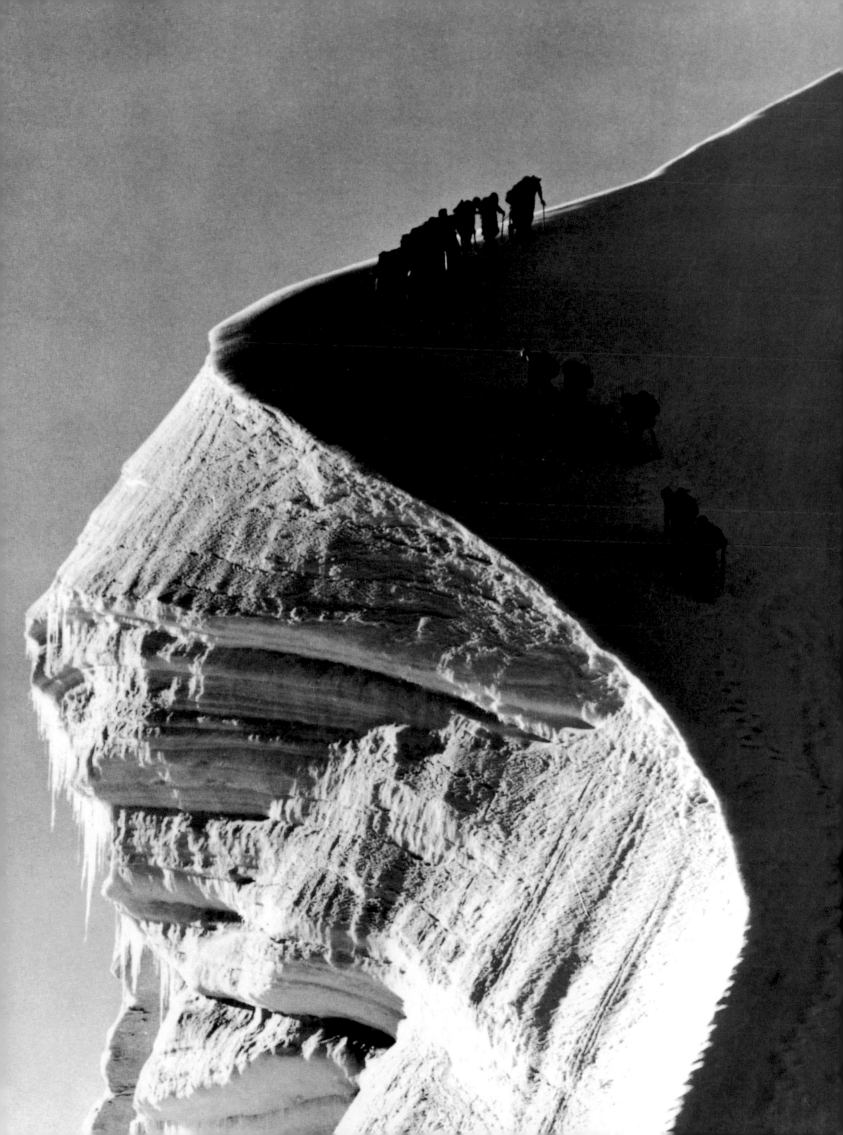

Above:

[16] Monsoon landscape in India.

Facing page:

[17] Cyclone in Java, Indonesia.

[18-19] Satellite photos of the Yang-Tse-Kiang, in China,
before and after the historic 1998 flood (*left:* May 27; *right:* August 12).

Previous pages:

[20] Flood in Baytown, Texas, USA,
photographed by Harald Sund for Life Magazine in July 1981.

Above:

[21] Corsica, 1965: learning to swim…

Facing page:

[22] Dani, Aix-les-Bains, photographed by Jacques-Henri Lartigue in August 1925.

Previous pages:

[27-28] Water ballets:

Left: Jupiter's Darling, 1955; *right:* Naïades, circa 1940.

Facing page:

[29] Sala, Biarritz, photographed by Jacques-Henri Lartigue, August 4, 1918.

[30] Hyères, at dawn. Photograph by Jacques-Henri Lartigue, 1929.

[31] Water games in New York
by Paul Himmel, 1950.

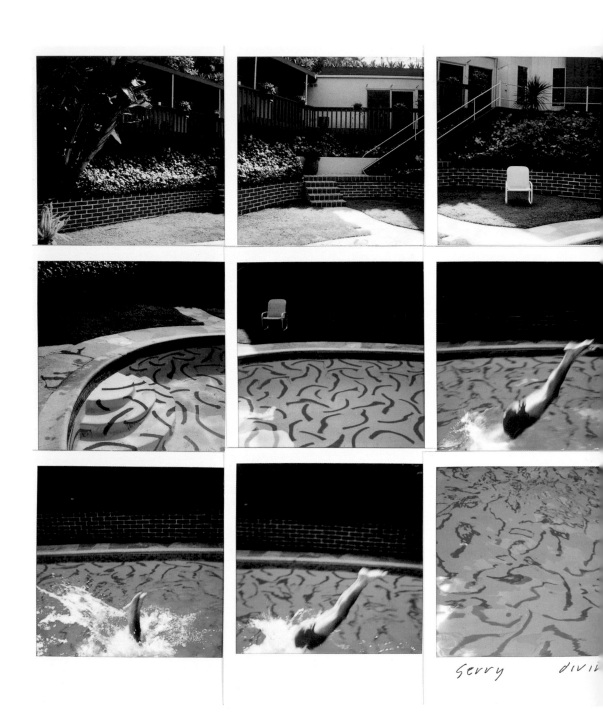

Serry   divil

Previous pages:

[35] Self-portrait as a fountain by Bruce Nauman,
taken from the series "Eleven Color Photographs", 1966-1967.

Above:

[36] Jerry diving, Sunday, Feb. 28th, 1982, by David Hockney.
Polaroids by Steve Oliver.

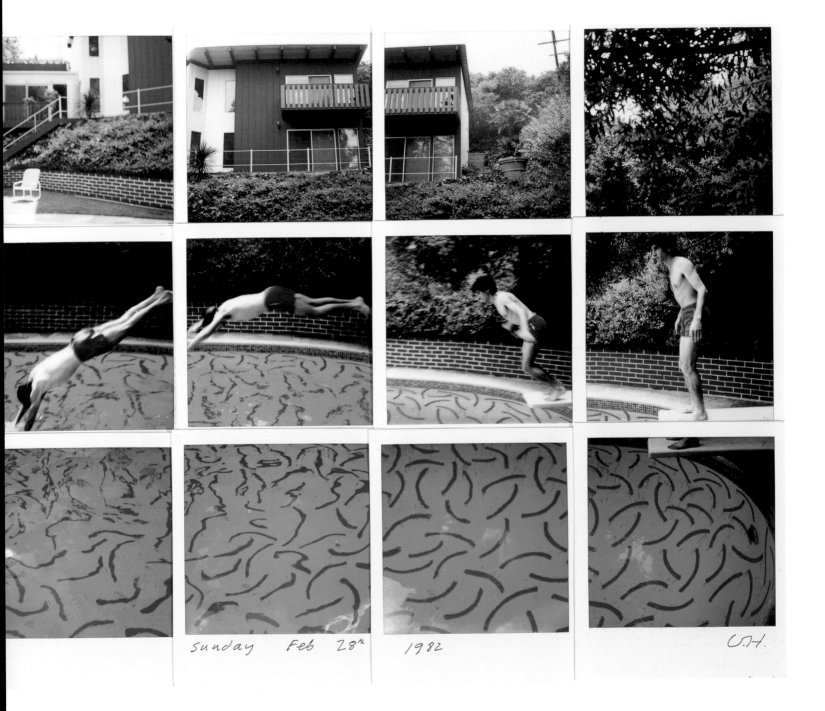

Sunday   Feb 28ª   1982   U.H.

[37] Underwater divers.
Photo essay by Mark Davidson.

[38] Irrigated terraced rice paddies, South Yunnan, China.

[39] Surrounded Islands, Biscayne Bay, Greater Miami, Florida,
Christo and Jeanne-Claude, 1980-1983.
603.85 m² of pink polypropylene surround the various natural elements of the site,
marking a new relationship between the earth, water, and inhabitants of Miami.

[40-41] Jean-Pierre Raynaud's pots submerged in the Red Sea, 1997.
Left: "Pink"; *right:* "Jaune".

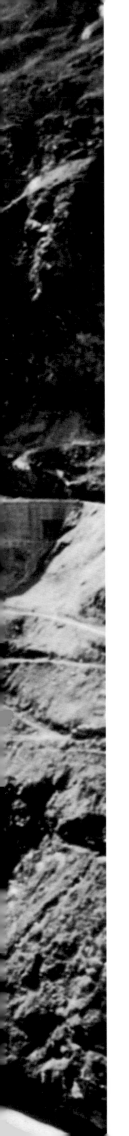

Facing page:

[42] Mauvoisin Dam, in Switzerland.

Following pages:

[43] Sea of Japan, Oki I, by Hiroshi Sugimoto, 1987.

[44] House of Water, work by Nils-Udo, 1982.
Spruce trunks, birch and willow branches (10.5 x 10.5 x 41 meters).
Wadden Sea, Cuxhaven (Holland).

Facing page:

[45] Reflections on running water.

Above:

[46] Snoqualmie Falls, Washington, USA.

Previous pages:

[47] Fisherman and water mill in the Guangxi Province, China.

Facing page:

[48] Swimming pool in Saint-Martin, Lesser Antilles, 1986.

Facing page:

[53] The Blue Lagoon,
by Virginia Beahan and Laura McPhee, 1988.
Geothermal pumping station built on the site
of Svartsengi (Island), known for its natural
hot springs.

Following pages:

[54] Dew. Temperature changes on Earth
cause the condensation of moisture in the air
into small droplets.

[55] Glass Tears. Man Ray
(Photographic Album, 1920-1934).

[61] Naomi Campbell photographed by Peter Lindbergh in 1992.

Above:

[62] Curious Moments. Caricature of a water cure in the early 1950s.

Facing page:

[63] Water-cure institution of Aix-les-Bains, in Savoie, France, in the early 1900s.

Above:

[64] "Water not for drinking". Fountain in Saint-Paul-de-Vence, France.

Facing page:

[65] Water-cure institution of Gellert, in Budapest, Hungary, 1983.

Facing page:

[66] The Crossing, 1996. Photo taken from a video installation by Bill Viola.

Above:

[67] Sacred, worshiped river and pilgrimage site, the Ganges in Benares, India.
The scattering of ashes is a good omen for future lives.

[68] Israel, January 5, 1954. Paul VI's visit to Lake Tiberias,
where, according to the Gospel, the miracle of the loaves and fishes took place.

Above:

[70] Subterranean reservoir in Montsouris, in Paris, built in 1874.
Diverted from the areas of Dreux, Sens, Provins, Nemours, and Fontainebleau,
Paris' water is funnelled via aqueducts to the city reservoirs.

Facing page:

[71] Water castle, Oregon, Ohio, USA, 1977.
Photo by Bernd and Hilla Becher.

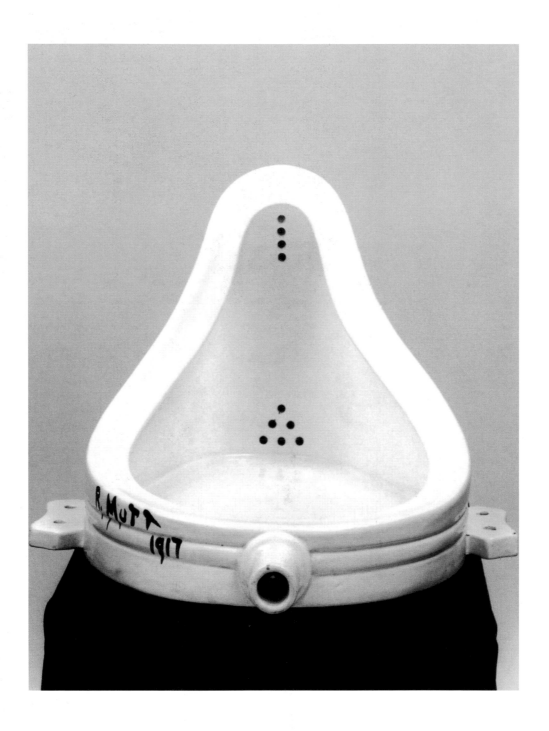

Above:

[72] Fountain, 1917, Marcel Duchamp.

Facing page:

[73] Spiral Jetty, Robert Smithson, 1970.
Rocks, salt crystals, earth, red water, algae (457 x 4.57 meters). Great Salt Lake, Utah, USA.

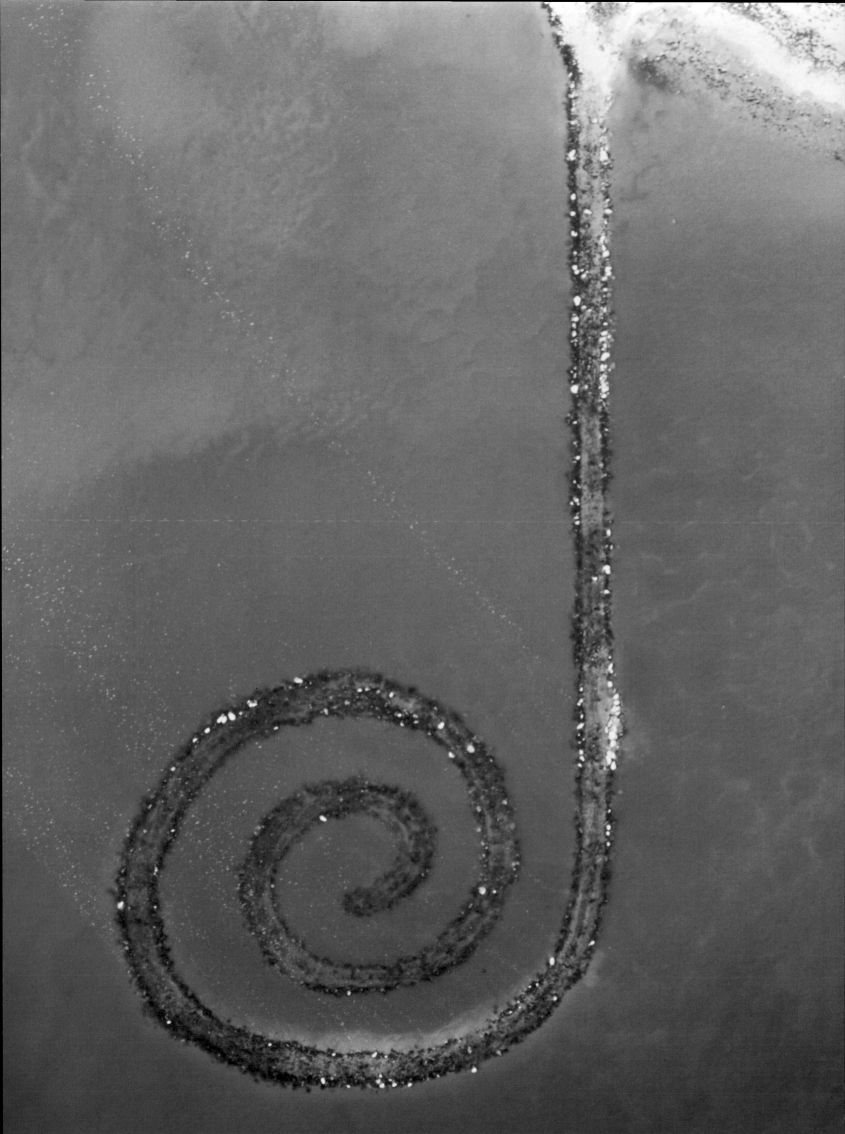

[74] Maharashtra, Bombay, India.
Scene from daily life during the monsoon, photographed by Carl de Keyzer in 1990.

Catalog

Principal natural mineral waters & spring waters of the world

The description of water composition allows one to measure its infinite diversity and uniqueness. The short monographs on the mineral waters and spring waters that follow reveal the extraordinary diversity of regions from which they emerge and the reason— aside from specific medical treatment—why one shouldn't always drink the same one!

Austria

GASTEINER

Mineral Water (Bad Gastein)

Origin: Gasteiner mineral water is bottled at the Bad Gastein thermal spa, in southwestern Austria, a site very much in vogue since the 19th century due to the frequent visits of Emperor Franz Joseph. Although this water emerges at a temperature of more than 104 °F, its mineral content is relatively low (107.9 mg/l). It is sold in still, sparkling and carbonated varieties. Gasteiner now belongs to the Brau AG group, and is the third best-selling water in Austria.

Composition (mg/l):		Indications:
Calcium:	24	Suitable for all diets.
Magnesium:	2.2	**Dominant flavors:**
Sodium:	15	Neutral water.
Potassium:	2.3	**Varieties:**
Sulphates:	34	Still, sparkling
Bicarbonates:	66.5	and carbonated.
Chloride:	7.2	
Nitrates:	/	
PH:	/	
Mineralization:	107.9	

GÜSSINGER

Mineral Water (Sulz)

Origin: Produced in southern Austria, Gussinger is a mineral water with an especially high concentration of minerals. Known since Roman times, it is mentioned publicly in 1469. Its reputation reached its peak under the Austro-Hungarian Empire, when the nobility went to taste it at its highly-prized thermal site. The marketing of this water began in 1956 and today has reached a annual production level of 40 million bottles. Gussinger mineral water is available in sparkling and carbonated varieties.

Composition (mg/l):		Indications:
Calcium:	114.6	Stimulates intestinal functions.
Magnesium:	24.6	
Sodium:	292.2	**Dominant flavors:**
Potassium:	15.8	Neutral water.
Sulphates:	5.8	**Varieties:**
Bicarbonates:	1.049.6	Sparkling and carbonated.
Chloride:	1.266	
Nitrates:	/	
PH:	/	
Mineralization:	1.683.2	

MARKUS QUELLE

Mineral Water (Pöttsching)

Origin: Markus Quelle mineral water is harnessed in Pottsching in a layer estimated to be 23,000 years old by an artesian well that reaches it 165 yards underground (a depth that protects it from all pollution). The company that sells it was founded in 1976 and its bottling began two years later. The factory was the first in Austria to adopt automated mineral water production. In 1988, it was absorbed by Romerquelle, the leader in Austrian mineral waters. Markus Quelle is lightly mineralized, with magnesium and remarkably balanced. With a sodium content of 44 mg/l, it is not recommended for strict sodium-free diets.

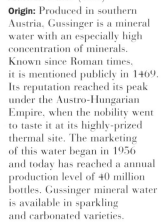

Composition (mg/l):		Indications:
Calcium:	94.6	Not suitable for low-sodium diets or baby bottle preparation.
Magnesium:	38.9	
Sodium:	44	
Potassium:	5.2	**Dominant flavors:**
Sulphates:	109.6	Neutral water.
Bicarbonates:	465	**Varieties:**
Chloride:	/	Sparkling and carbonated.
Nitrates:	/	
PH:	7	
Mineralization:	/	

RÖMERQUELLE

Mineral Water (Edelstal)

Origin: The Edelsal spring, located 37.5 miles east of Vienna, was already known 2,000 years ago when Roman Emperor Marcus Aurelius lived in the neighboring garrison of Cornuntum. This 5,000-year-old natural mineral water, protected from pollution by impermeable layers, bubbles up from an artesian well 437 yd deep. Moderately mineralized, it is rich in calcium, magnesium and sulphates. Its sodium content is only 13.9 mg/l. With no nitrates, it is remarkably pure, but its mineralization of 1,007 mg/l and its richness in sulphates makes it inappropriate for infants. However, it is perfectly suited to sodium-free diets.

Composition (mg/l):		Indications:
Calcium:	146.4	Suitable for low-sodium diets; not suitable for baby bottle preparation.
Magnesium:	65.6	
Sodium:	13.9	
Potassium:	2	**Dominant flavors:**
Sulphates:	298.6	Neutral water.
Bicarbonates:	/	**Varieties:**
Chloride:	8	Still, sparkling
Nitrates:	0.5	and carbonated.
PH:	5.7	
Mineralization:	1.007	

SEVERIN QUELLE

Mineral Water

Origin: In production since 1974. Severin Quelle natural mineral water belongs to Brau A.G. A mineral water with a relatively high mineral content (1.707 mg/l). Severin Quelle is especially recommended for the stimulation of renal and intestinal functions. It is often used to create the traditional Austrian drink, the Spritzer, a blend of wine and mineral water.

Composition (mg/l):		Indications:
Calcium:	112.6	Stimulates renal and intestinal functions.
Magnesium:	30.6	
Sodium:	293.7	**Dominant flavors:**
Potassium:	14.7	Neutral water.
Sulphates:	10.1	**Variety:**
Bicarbonates:	1.025	Carbonated.
Chloride:	151.5	
Nitrates:	/	
PH:	/	
Mineralization:	1.707	

MONTES

Mineral Water (Tyrol. Alps)

Origin: In western Austria, the Tyrol mountains have a wide array of natural mineral waters that have been known since Roman times. Montes comes directly from the Alps, which filter the precious mineral salts all the way from the source. The water retains a mineral content and an unchanging purity. A new mineral water in the market place, Montes began production in 1992. It is distributed in sparkling and carbonated varieties.

Composition (mg/l):		Indications:
Calcium:	111.2	Suitable for all diets.
Magnesium:	50.4	**Dominant flavors:**
Sodium:	20.8	Neutral water, with an acidic tendency.
Potassium:	4.2	
Sulphates:	260.6	**Varieties:**
Bicarbonates:	275.1	Sparkling and carbonated.
Chloride:	20.7	
Nitrates:	1.7	
PH:	5.1	
Mineralization:	/	

Belgium

BRU
Mineral Water (Ardennes)

Origin: The Bru springs appeared on Roman maps under the name Fontes Acidi. In the Middle Ages, the monks of the Stavelot-Malmedy abbey came to pump the water for their personal consumption. Bru water was sold as early as the seventeenth century, but its industrial harnessing and bottling began only in 1903. The site is located in a 13 miles² zone that is protected from pollution. After running slowly across the sandstone and carbonated shale, the naturally carbonated water is pumped from a deep layer, degasified, deferred and filtered, then regasified with its own gas. Lightly mineralized, it is low in sodium and contains a small amount of fluor (0.2 mg/l).

Composition (mg/l):		Indications:
Calcium:	21	Suitable for low-sodium diets.
Magnesium:	20	**Dominant flavors:**
Sodium:	8	Impression
Potassium:	1.5	of freshness (said to be half-sparkling).
Sulphates:	5	**Variety:**
Bicarbonates:	15	Carbonated.
Chloride:	4	
Nitrates:	/	
PH:	5	
Mineralization:	/	

DUKE
Mineral Water (Ardennes)

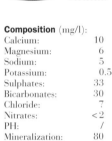

Origin: The Duke spring was discovered around 1950, near the famous Formula 1 automobile circuit in Spa-Francorchamps. Lightly mineralized (80 mg/l) and very pure (less than 2 mg/l of nitrates). Duke natural mineral water contains only 5 mg/l of sodium, making it ideal for those on the strictest sodium-free diets and for the preparation of food for infants. It has an annual production of 14 million liters. Duke mineral water is distributed in still, carbonated and sparkling versions.

Composition (mg/l):		Indications:
Calcium:	10	Suitable for strict sodium-free diets and baby bottle preparation.
Magnesium:	6	
Sodium:	5	
Potassium:	0.5	**Dominant flavors:**
Sulphates:	33	Neutral water.
Bicarbonates:	30	**Varieties:**
Chloride:	7	Still, carbonated and sparkling.
Nitrates:	<2	
PH:	/	
Mineralization:	80	

SPA BARISART
Mineral Water (Ardennes)

Origin: Spa Barisart is a natural mineral water made gaseous by the addition of carbonic gas (6.4 g/l). The Barisart spring, known to some by the name Mambaye, is located to the south of the city of Spa, at an elevation of about 330 yd. in the pool pouring from the Meyerbeer stream. The water from this spring was chosen to be gasified because its mineral content is a bit higher than that of the Reine. Its harnessing necessitated digging a very long gallery—over 660 yd long. Spa Barisart, poor in minerals (49 mg/l), contains 10 mg/l of silica. Its nitrate content, like those of the other waters of Spa, is very low (1.5 mg/l).

Composition (mg/l):		Indications:
Calcium:	5.5	Not suitable for baby bottle preparation.
Magnesium:	1.3	
Sodium:	5	**Dominant flavors:**
Potassium:	0.5	Lightly acidic; rather big bubbles.
Sulphates:	7.5	**Variety:**
Bicarbonates:	18	Carbonated.
Chloride:	5.5	
Nitrates:	/	
PH:	4.1	
Mineralization:	/	

SPA MARIE-HENRIETTE
Mineral Water (Ardennes)

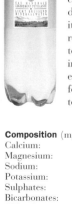

Origin: Spa Marie-Henriette is a naturally gaseous mineral water. Its spring, ferruginous and carbogaseous, is located in a wooded area northeast of Spa, in the Niveze region, upstream from Warfaaz Lake. It emerges naturally gaseous into an underground chamber, at one extremity of an 95-yard tunnel (thanks to the boring done in 1866 and improved upon since). Of deep origins, naturally enriched with carbonic gas resulting from the decomposition of carbonates, it dissolves the minerals of the rocks along which it runs as it rises toward the ground and thus gathers iron and manganese. Reserved exclusively for mineral bath cures for a long time, it only began to be sold in bottles in 1992.

Composition (mg/l):		Indications:
Calcium:	11	Suitable for low-sodium diets.
Magnesium:	7	
Sodium:	10.5	**Dominant flavors:**
Potassium:	1.3	Freshness; small bubbles.
Sulphates:	6.5	**Variety:**
Bicarbonates:	75	Carbonated.
Chloride:	9.5	
Nitrates:	/	
PH:	4.9	
Mineralization:	/	

SPONTIN DUCHESSE
Mineral Water (Namur province)

Origin: The Spontin spring's virtues have been known since Antiquity. This Namur village is located at the end of a valley rimmed with rocky and wooded hills, at the edge of a waterway (the Bocq). At the end of the 19th century, the first tests were done, among them the Duchesse spring (the name dates back to feudal times): thanks to its "good water", the long time sterile wife of the Lord of Spontin could have a child. Sold since 1928, Duchesse was recognized as a mineral water by the Royal Academy of Medicine in 1939. Rich in bicarbonates and calcium and lightly mineralized, with a very low sodium content, it has diuretic properties and facilitates digestion.

Composition (mg/l):		Indications:
Calcium:	82	Suitable for low-sodium diets and baby bottle preparation (still water).
Magnesium:	10	
Sodium:	6	
Potassium:	1.5	**Dominant flavors:**
Sulphates:	32	Neutral water.
Bicarbonates:	240	**Varieties:**
Chloride:	17	Still and carbonated.
Nitrates:	/	
PH:	7.7	
Mineralization:	/	

VALVERT
Mineral Water (Ardennes)

Origin: Valvert mineral water has its spring in southern Ardennes, not far from the frontier with the Luxembourg, in the heart of a protected 13.5-miles² forest, far from all industrial and agricultural pollution. It was discovered recently (in 1993). The Perrier-Vittel company (Nestle group) did everything they could to keep the exceptional site intact. Very much a presence in both France and Belgium, it is also sold in other European countries (and in Asia). Lightly mineralized, it can be consumed by all without restriction.

Composition (mg/l):		Indications:
Calcium:	67.6	Suitable for all sodium-free diets and baby bottle preparation.
Magnesium:	2	
Sodium:	1.9	
Potassium:	0.2	**Dominant flavors:**
Sulphates:	18	Fluid and light, refreshing aftertaste.
Bicarbonates:	204	**Variety:**
Chloride:	4	Still.
Nitrates:	3.5	
PH:	7.3	
Mineralization:	201	

Canada

DIVA
Spring Water (Quebec)

Origin: Cetobel Inc. has been in operation in Quebec since 1993. This company bottles its own brand, Diva, as well as other brands for private distribution. Diva is essentially destined for export—its sale began in 1996. To preserve its purity, Diva natural spring water is bottled without filtration for a water virtually lacking in minerals (130 mg/l).

Composition (mg/l):	
Calcium:	31
Magnesium:	7
Sodium:	3
Potassium:	0
Sulphates:	16
Bicarbonates:	125
Chloride:	3
Nitrates:	3
PH:	/
Mineralization:	130

Indications:
Suitable for low-sodium diets.
Dominant flavors:
Light taste.
Variety:
Still.

MONTCLAIR
Mineral Water (Quebec)

Origin: This national brand groups together five Canadian springs in the Quebec province. Discovered in 1880, these gaseous waters are more or less mineralized depending on their spring. Two gaseous waters from the Saint-Joseph and Saint-Lazare springs are bottled under the Montclair name.

Composition (mg/l):	
Calcium:	41
Magnesium:	3
Sodium:	2
Potassium:	0
Sulphates:	2
Bicarbonates:	134
Chloride:	3
Nitrates:	3
PH:	8
Mineralization:	139

Indications:
Suitable for all diets.
Dominant flavors:
Neutral and refreshing water.
Variety:
Carbonated.

SAINT-JUSTIN
Spring Water (Quebec)

Origin: The Saint-Justin spring, discovered in 1895, was known until 1976 by the name of the village where it is located, in the Maskinonge county. It originates in the mountainous region of the Lower-Laurentides. Over the course of its journey, Saint-Justin spring water gathers minerals (1,000 mg/l) and particularly bicarbonates (560 mg/l).

Composition (mg/l):	
Calcium:	7
Magnesium:	6
Sodium:	415
Potassium:	3
Sulphates:	0
Bicarbonates:	560
Chloride:	350
Nitrates:	0
PH:	/
Mineralization:	1,000

Indications:
Digestive properties.
Dominant flavors:
Mildly sparkling and light.
Variety:
Carbonated.

WOTTON
Spring Water (Quebec)

Origin: The water from the Wotton spring in Quebec belongs to Cetobel Inc. It came on the market in 1996, primarily for local distribution.

Composition (mg/l):	
Calcium:	31
Magnesium:	7
Sodium:	3
Potassium:	0
Sulphates:	16
Bicarbonates:	125
Chloride:	3
Nitrates:	3
PH:	/
Mineralization:	130

Indications:
Suitable for low-sodium diets.
Dominant flavors:
Very light.
Variety:
Still.

France

ARVIE
Mineral Water (Puy-de-Dome)

Origin: Arvie mineral water emerges naturally gaseous in Ardes, on the Couze, between the Cantal and Mont-Dore mountains, in an area protected by the Auvergne Volcanic natural park. It acquires its minerals progressively along the crystalline rocks of the Cezailler plateau and emerges without a trace of nitrates. Recognized as a natural mineral water in 1884, it is rich in mineral salts (2,520 mg/l), bicarbonates, calcium, sodium and chloride, with high magnesium and potassium contents. Fairly rich in fluor, it is useful in the fight against tooth decay. Ideal for adults, it is too sodic (650 mg/l) for those restricted by a sodium-free diet or for baby bottle preparation.

Composition (mg/l):		Indications:
Calcium:	170	Not suitable for
Magnesium:	92	sodium-free diets,
Sodium:	650	baby bottle
Potassium:	130	preparation or pregnant
Sulphates:	31	women.
Bicarbonates:	2,195	**Dominant flavors:**
Chloride:	387	Sparkling
Nitrates:	0	and salty taste.
PH:	/	**Variety:** Carbonated.
Mineralization:	2,520	

BADOIT
Mineral Water (Loire)

Origin: The Romans built thermal mineral baths (of which traces remain) in Saint-Galmier, above the Forez plain. It is there that the naturally-gaseous mineral water that doctors of the region have appreciated for its curative properties since the 18th century emerges. These properties were confirmed in 1898 when the Academie de Medecine recognized it as a national asset. A moderately mineralized water (1,200 mg/l), with bicarbonates, calcium, magnesium, degasified and regasified with its own gas, Badoit facilitates digestion. Its fluor content (1 mg/l) allows it to play a role in the fight against tooth decay. It has belonged to the Societe des eaux minerales d'Evian since 1965 and is owned by the Danone group.

Composition (mg/l):		Indications:
Calcium:	190	Aids digestion.
Magnesium:	85	Not suitable for baby
Sodium:	150	bottle preparation.
Potassium:	10	**Dominant flavors:**
Sulphates:	40	Pleasantly
Bicarbonates:	1,300	sparkling taste.
Chloride:	40	**Variety:**
Nitrates:	/	Carbonated.
PH:	6	
Mineralization:	1,200	

CAROLA
Spring Water (Alsace)

Origin: In 1888, Doctor Chretien Staub, whose wife's name was Caroline—from which Carola is derived—developed an interest in a spring known since the sixteenth century as the "castle spring". It emerges in Ribeauville (Upper Rhine), the "village of three castles", appreciated for its wines and excellent climate and deemed worthy to be classed as a health resort in 1995. The water emerges at a temperature of 65 °F, after a slow progression along the alluvial deposits of the quaternary, a gauge of its purity and mineralization (less than 1,500 mg/l). Carola is part of the Perrier-Vittel group (Nestle).

Composition (mg/l):		Indications:
Calcium:	83	Suitable for baby bottle
Magnesium:	24	preparation (still water).
Sodium:	114	**Dominant flavors:**
Potassium:	7	Very light touch
Sulphates:	136	of bitterness.
Bicarbonates:	414	**Varieties:**
Chloride:	57	Still, sparkling,
Nitrates:	1	and carbonated (natural
PH:	6.8	and flavored).
Mineralization:	645	

CHATELDON
Mineral Water (Puy-de-Dôme)

Origin: The glory of Chateldon mineral water dates back to 1650, the year in which Fagon, court doctor, recommended it to Louis XIV: "The waters of Chateldon will cure Your Majesty sometimes, will sooth Him often and console Him always." Convinced, the Sun King had it brought to him (on the backs of mules). The royal road did not end there for Chateldon: in 1778, Dr. Desbest, consultant to Louis XV and army doctor, described it in a work as "the lightest and most digestible water in the Kingdom". Emerging from the Sergentale spring, Chateldon is moderately mineralized, with bicarbonates, calcium and sodium, fluoridated and without nitrates.

Composition (mg/l):		Indications:
Calcium:	383	Not suitable for
Magnesium:	49	sodium-free diets.
Sodium:	240	**Dominant flavors:**
Potassium:	35	Fresh taste
Sulphates:	20	and small bubbles.
Bicarbonates:	2,075	**Variety:**
Chloride:	7	Carbonated.
Nitrates:	0	
PH:	6.2	
Mineralization:	1,882	

CONTREX
Mineral Water (Vosges)

Origin: The small valley of Contrexville is located at the foot of the Vosges mountain range. The known origin of Contrexville dates back to the thirteenth century but its water had been appreciated since long before then, during the Gallo-Roman era. A first mineral bath spa was built in 1774. Contrex was officially recognized as a natural mineral water in 1861. The spa attained even greater success and all the aristocracy of Europe rushed to go there. Rich in mineral salts (2,125 mg/l), sulphated, with calcium and magnesium, Contrex can be consumed daily by one and all (with the exception of infants). It is recognized for its diuretic properties.

Composition (mg/l):		Indications:
Calcium:	486	Suitable for
Magnesium:	84	low-sodium diets.
Sodium:	9.1	**Dominant flavors:**
Potassium:	3.2	Alkaline, with a slightly
Sulphates:	1,187	bitter aftertaste.
Bicarbonates:	403	**Variety:**
Chloride:	8.6	Still.
Nitrates:	2.7	
PH:	7.2	
Mineralization:	2,125	

CRISTALINE
SAINT-CYR LA SOURCE
Spring Water (Loire)

Origin: Registered in 1984, the water of Saint-Cyr la Source has been exploited by the Compagnie generale des eaux de source (General company of Spring Waters) since 1985. Pumped some 165 yd underground near Orleans, this lightly mineralized spring water (300 mg/l) contains virtually no nitrates (1 mg/l), allowing it to be recommended in the preparation of food for infants.

Composition (mg/l):		Indications:
Calcium:	7.1	Suitable for the strictest
Magnesium:	9.5	sodium-free and baby
Sodium:	11.2	bottle preparation.
Potassium:	3.2	**Dominant flavors:**
Sulphates:	<5	Neutral water.
Bicarbonates:	250	**Variety:**
Chloride:	20	Still.
Nitrates:	1	
PH:	7.45	
Mineralization:	300	

ÉVIAN

Mineral Water (Haute-Savoie)

Origin: The Marquis of L'Essert came to take the waters in Amphion-les-Bains, near Evian, in 1789. Anxious to cure his gravel (urinary stones), he followed the recommendations of those in Evian and drank the water from the Sainte-Catherine fountain several days in a row. This limpid and "well-passing" water having assuaged his suffering, he spread word of its healing power. The owner of the fountain, named Cachat, decided to enclose it and sell the water. In 1826, the Duke of Savo granted the right for it to be bottled. After the re-unification of Savo with France, this authorization was confirmed. The water of Evian (the Cachat spring), weakly mineralized and low in sodium, is recommended for sodium-free diets and baby bottle preparation.

Composition (mg/l):		Indications:
Calcium:	78	Suitable for all diets, including sodium-free diets and baby bottle preparation.
Magnesium:	24	
Sodium:	5	
Potassium:	1	**Dominant flavors:**
Sulphates:	10	Neutral taste, water of reference.
Bicarbonates:	357	
Chloride:	4.5	**Variety:**
Nitrates:	3.8	Still.
PH:	7.2	
Mineralization:	309	

HÉPAR

Mineral Water (Vosges)

Origin: The spring water known today by the name of Hepar is harnessed in the western part of the Vosges basin, on the calcareous and marl Vittel plateau where abundant rains contribute to the replenishment of the layer. Discovered in 1873, 1.8 mile east of Vittel, it was baptized as a salted spring due to its great richness in mineral salts. Recognized as a natural mineral water in 1875 and a national asset in 1903, it was renamed Hepar in 1920 to underline its therapeutic properties. It is one of the still French waters that is richest in magnesium. It is recommended for people deficient in magnesium and useful in fighting against constipation and migraines.

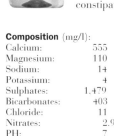

Composition (mg/l):		Indications:
Calcium:	555	Not suitable for baby bottle preparation.
Magnesium:	110	
Sodium:	14	**Dominant flavors:**
Potassium:	4	Rocky taste and mineral smell.
Sulphates:	1,479	
Bicarbonates:	403	**Variety:**
Chloride:	11	Still.
Nitrates:	2.9	
PH:	7	
Mineralization:	2,580	

MONT ROUCOUS

Mineral Water (Tarn)

Origin: This spring was discovered in 1973 in the Lacaune mountains national forest, in the Haut-Languedoc natural park—its name means "mountain of small stones" in Occitan.
It was probably known by the Romans because the remains of a Gallo-Roman pool were found in the area. Emerging from granite rocks at an elevation of 1,014 yd, it was initially marketed as a "spring water" before being registered as a "natural mineral water" in 1993. Mont Roucous water is without a doubt the least mineralized water of all the mineral waters of Europe (19 mg/l). Its diuretic properties are recognized and its high silica content (6.9 mg/l) allows it to be recommended in the fight against atherosclerosis.

Composition (mg/l):		Indications:
Calcium:	1.2	Suitable for sodium-free diets and baby bottle preparation.
Magnesium:	0.2	
Sodium:	2.8	
Potassium:	0.4	**Dominant flavors:**
Sulphates:	3.3	Mildly acidic.
Bicarbonates:	4.9	**Variety:**
Chloride:	3.2	Still.
Nitrates:	2.3	
PH:	6	
Mineralization:	19	

MONTCALM

Spring Water (Pyrenees)

Origin: Montcalm mountain spring water is harnessed without pumping at an elevation of more than 1,093 yd in the heart of the Ariege region of the Pyrenees. Filtered along its passage through the quartz and granite rocks, it is remarkably pure and contains a very low amount of nitrates (0.8 mg/l). Among the least mineralized spring waters (28 mg/l), it is particularly suitable for the preparation of food for infants (it is the only bottled water in France to carry the notice "water intended for infants"), daily consumption by pregnant women and for those restricted to a low-sodium diet. Montcalm spring water is the first spring water to be sold in France in 5 liter bottles, a process started in 1998.

Composition (mg/l):		Indications:
Calcium:	2.7	Suitable for sodium-free diets and baby bottle preparation.
Magnesium:	0.6	
Sodium:	1.3	
Potassium:	0.3	**Dominant flavors:**
Sulphates:	9.4	Mild bitter.
Bicarbonates:	1.8	**Variety:**
Chloride:	0.5	Still.
Nitrates:	0.8	
PH:	6.8	
Mineralization:	28	

PERRIER

Mineral Water (Gard)

Origin: Located in Vergeze near Nimes, the Perrier spring was first discovered by the Romans. With the volcanic influence that causes the mineral water to emerge bubbling, the spring long retained its appellation "Bouillens". Dr. Perrier decided to market it in 1863 thanks to the support of Sir St John Harmsworth. The latter was inspired to give the bottle its famous shape by his Indian gymnastics clubs. Weak in minerals, Perrier owes its unique flavor and thirst-quenching character to the force of its bubbles. Rich in bicarbonates and calcium. Perrier is regasified with its own gas. It is without a doubt the most carbonated mineral water sold in the world; it is among the top three brands of food products in the world.

Composition (mg/l):		Indications:
Calcium:	147	Suitable for all diets.
Magnesium:	3	**Dominant flavors:**
Sodium:	9	Impression of freshness, enduring bubbles, mildly bitter taste.
Potassium:	1.1	
Sulphates:	33	
Bicarbonates:	390	**Variety:**
Chloride:	22	Carbonated.
Nitrates:	18	
PH:	5	
Mineralization:	447	

PIERVAL

Spring Water (Eure)

Origin: This spring water emerges in Pont-Saint-Pierre, a village located in a green valley 16 miles from Rouen, in the corner of a castle park dating back to the end of the 14th century, nicknamed by the Peripontains "Gabrielle's castle" in memory of the visit made by Henry IV's favorite, Gabrielle d'Estrees, during the English siege of Rouen. This pure and light water, reputed since the fifteenth century to give long life, has always been enjoyed by the inhabitants of the village. Its sale under the name of Pierval began in 1959 in elegant glass bottles. In the sixties, Pierval was the second brand to adopt plastic bottles. Today it exports over half of what it produces.

Composition (mg/l):		Indications:
Calcium:	104	Suitable for sodium-free diets and baby bottle preparation.
Magnesium:	4	
Sodium:	8	
Potassium:	0.8	**Dominant flavors:**
Sulphates:	8	Thirst-quenching, with a clearly mineral taste.
Bicarbonates:	314	
Chloride:	13.6	**Variety:**
Nitrates:	12	Still.
PH:	7.2	
Mineralization:	331	

QUÉZAC

Mineral Water (Gard)

Origin: This naturally bubbly mineral water emerges in the heart of Lozère near the village of Quézac, against the Causse Mejean cliffs, about 19 miles from Mende. Already enjoyed by the Celts, the Quezac spring, reputed for its miraculous cures, became a pilgrims destination for in the eleventh century. In 1859, Dr. Comandre had the first harnessing installations put in place. Its exploitation was performed by hand for almost a century and a half and finally began on its current size taking in 1995. Rich in bicarbonates, sodium, calcium and magnesium, its fluor content is useful in the fight against tooth decay.

Composition (mg/l):		Indications:
Calcium:	241	Aids digestion;
Magnesium:	95	not suitable for sodium-
Sodium:	255	free diets.
Potassium:	49.7	**Dominant flavors:**
Sulphates:	143	Small bubbles.
Bicarbonates:	1,685.4	**Variety:**
Chloride:	38	Carbonated.
Nitrates:	<1	
PH:	6.1	
Mineralization:	1,656	

SAINT-AMAND

Mineral Water (Nord)

Origin: Saint-Amand mineral water was already known during the Celtic era. It emerges in the heart of a regional natural park in Saint-Amand-des-Eaux, a site preserved from all outside pollution. Harnessed at a depth of over 98 yd, with a flow of 1,308 yd³/h, it is moderately mineralized, rich in calcium, fluoridated (2 mg/l) and contains no nitrates. A diuretic, it is also recommended for growing children and contributes to the prevention of tooth decay. The sparkling version is obtained by the addition of carbonic gas. The Saint-Amand group, fourth France's mineral water producer, was the first to sell its spring water in 5 liter containers.

Composition (mg/l):		Indications:
Calcium:	176	Suitable for all diets
Magnesium:	46	and baby bottle preparation;
Sodium:	28	recommended for growth.
Potassium:	6	**Dominant flavors:**
Sulphates:	372	Neutral water.
Bicarbonates:	312	**Varieties:**
Chloride:	40	Plain still, flavored still
Nitrates:	0	and carbonated.
PH:	7	
Mineralization:	889	

SAINT-ANTONIN

Mineral Water (Aveyron)

Origin: The Black Prince spring is harnessed in a perfectly protected area in the gorges of the Aveyron, near the village of Saint-Antonin, at the confluence of the Aveyron and Bonnette, built on the site of the Merovingian Nobleval, where Pepin le Bref founded an abbey in 763. The Black Prince spring was bought by the Saint-Amand group in 1998, France's fourth mineral-water producer. Saint-Antonin mineral water is rich in bicarbonates, calcium, magnesium and sulphates and contains a relatively high fluor content (1.3 mg/l), allowing it to contribute to the prevention of tooth decay. Its sulphate content favors the elimination of toxins.

Composition (mg/l):		Indications:
Calcium:	528	Suitable for people
Magnesium:	78	on a diet.
Sodium:	9	**Dominant flavors:**
Potassium:	3	Slightly salty
Sulphates:	1,342	taste with a bitter edge.
Bicarbonates:	329	**Variety:**
Chloride:	9	Still.
Nitrates:	0	
PH:	7.1	
Mineralization:	1,800	

SAINT-YORRE

Mineral Water (Allier)

Origin: Pharmacist Nicholas Larbaud, the owner of a marshy piece of land in Saint-Yorre (a small town in the Vichy basin) obtained the right to sell his water in the middle of the nineteenth century. His example was then followed: by 1930 more than 140 springs had been drilled. Today, all the water from these springs is treated in a single bottling plant and sold under the same "Saint-Yorre" label. A sodic, chloridated and rich in bicarbonates water, strongly mineralized, decanted and regasified with its own gas, Saint-Yorre has a very high fluor content (9 mg/l). It is useful in the treatment of liver problems and biliary tracts. Very rich in sodium, it is not recommended for those on a sodium-free diet.

Composition (mg/l):		Indications:
Calcium:	90	Not suitable for low-sodium
Magnesium:	11	diets or small children.
Sodium:	1,708	**Dominant flavors:**
Potassium:	132	Chemical smell
Sulphates:	174	and salty taste.
Bicarbonates:	4,368	**Variety:**
Chloride:	322	Carbonated.
Nitrates:	<1	
PH:	6.6	
Mineralization:	4,774	

SALVETAT

Mineral Water (Hérault)

Origin: This gaseous mineral water, rich in bicarbonates and calcium, emerges at an elevation of 711 yd from the Rieumajou spring, in the heart of the Upper-Languedoc natural park, 41 miles from Béziers. It originates with the rains that seep into the cristalline and metamorphic rocks that filter it and give it its minerals. The pilgrims on their way to Saint-James-of-Compostella enjoyed it. Recognized as a mineral water in 1848, it was bottled until 1930, then abandoned due to the construction of Raviege Lake. It resumed operation after its purchase in 1990 by the Société des eaux minérales d'Évian (Danone group). Degasified, it is then regasified with its own gas.

Composition (mg/l):		Indications:
Calcium:	253	Suitable for
Magnesium:	11	low-sodium diets.
Sodium:	7	**Dominant flavors:**
Potassium:	3	Mild, light taste,
Sulphates:	25	effervescence, small
Bicarbonates:	820	bubbles.
Chloride:	4	**Variety:**
Nitrates:	<1	Carbonated.
PH:	6	
Mineralization:	850	

THONON

Mineral Water (Haute-Savoie)

Origin: During the work that went into harnessing it (1882), Gallo-Roman ruins were discovered proving that water from the Versoie spring, tapped near Thonon on the borders of Lake Geneva, was enjoyed as early as Antiquity. In the sixteenth century, François de Sales, Bishop of Geneva, spread word of its virtues. In 1852, Miss Josephine Antoinette de Lort made a gift of it to the city of Thonon. The spring was recognized as a national asset in 1864 and a mineral bath spa was built there from 1886 to 1888. During its slow course along the fine sands and gravel emanating from the granite and eruptive rocks, the water undergoes a perfect filtration and acquires its weak mineral content. A diuretic, it is suitable for care of the urinary system.

Composition (mg/l):		Indications:
Calcium:	108	Suitable for sodium-free
Magnesium:	14	diets and baby bottle
Sodium:	3	preparation.
Potassium:	<1	**Dominant flavors:**
Sulphates:	13	No dominant.
Bicarbonates:	350	**Variety:**
Chloride:	9	Still.
Nitrates:	12	
PH:	7.4	
Mineralization:	342	

VERNIÈRE

Mineral Water (Hérault)

Origin: The Vernière spring is located in a small village, at the foot of the Cevennes, at the entrance to the Upper Languedoc regional natural park, 25 miles from Béziers and 19 miles from Montpellier. It is said to have emerged when the mining galleries were sunk. Its virtues, according to the legend, were supposed to have been discovered by accident during the seventeenth century, when a peasant suffering from pain was cured after having bathed in the muddy marsh that it had created. Napoleon III authorized its sale in 1861. Vernière spring water, rich in bicarbonates, calcium, magnesium, moderately mineralized and very diuretic, is bottled after having been degasified and regasified with its own gas. 0.5 mile of the Lamalou-les-Bains mineral bath spa.

Composition (mg/l):
Calcium:	190	
Magnesium:	72	
Sodium:	154	
Potassium:	49	
Sulphates:	158	
Bicarbonates:	1.170	
Chloride:	18	
Nitrates:	0	
PH:	6	
Mineralization:	1.226	

Indications:
Not suitable for low-sodium diets.
Dominant flavors:
Small bubbles.
Variety:
Carbonated.

VICHY CÉLESTINS

Mineral Water (Allier)

Origin: Vichy water was already known in the Gallo-Roman era. In the fifteenth century, Louis de Bourbon spread word of its qualities and founded the Celestine convent. In the seventeenth century, Madame de Sévigné took the waters there. She writes: "One had to be seen in Vichy to be recognized, we took our girls there to marry them off..." In the nineteenth century, Napoleon III came to cure his rheumatism, gout and skin ailments. In 1863, an imperial decree recognized the Celestine spring as a national asset. Of the fourteen springs in Vichy, only Vichy Celestins is bottled after having been degasified and regasified. Rich in bicarbonates, sodium and chloride, it has a high level of minerals (3,325 mg/l) and is very rich in fluor (6 mg/l).

Composition (mg/l):
Calcium:	103	
Magnesium:	10	
Sodium:	1.172	
Potassium:	66	
Sulphates:	138	
Bicarbonates:	2.939	
Chloride:	235	
Nitrates:	0	
PH:	6.8	
Mineralization:	3.325	

Indications:
Not suitable for sodium-free diets, baby bottle preparation, or young children.
Dominant flavors:
Strong flavor and salty taste.
Variety:
Carbonated.

VITTEL

Mineral Water (Vosges)

Origin: The small city of Vittel, in the western part of the Vosges, owes its name to the Roman general Aulus Vietelius (15-69), commander of the Lower German army, put to death by the people of Rome shortly after having been proclaimed emperor. The first mineral bath spa in Vittel was opened in 1855—the sale of the Grande Source began the same year. In 1903, the Académie de Médecine officially gave its approval and recognized its curative properties, especially for "gout, gravel, diabetes, dyspepsia and urinary tracts". High in sulphates and calcium, but containing little sodium, it is suitable for sodium-free diets. La Société Générale des eaux minérales de Vittel, founded in 1882, today belongs to the Nestlé group.

Composition (mg/l):
Calcium:	202	
Magnesium:	36	
Sodium:	3.8	
Potassium:	2	
Sulphates:	306	
Bicarbonates:	402	
Chloride:	7.2	
Nitrates:	6	
PH:	7.2	
Mineralization:	841	

Indications:
Suitable for sodium-free diets.
Dominant flavors:
Mineral smell, mild saline point, and light bitterness.
Variety:
Still.

VOLVIC

Mineral Water (Auvergne)

Origin: Volvic mineral water arrived on the market later than most other French mineral waters because its spring was only discovered in 1963. Classed as a natural mineral water in 1965, it is pumped on the slope of the Puys chain, at the heart of the Auvergne regional natural volcanic park, 7.5 miles from Clermont-Ferrand, the main city in the Puy-de-Dome department. Its rise to success was rapid because is production level is not far from reaching a million liters annually. Volvic is weak in minerals (109 mg/l), low in calcium, contains only a small amount of sodium, is very diuretic and is particularly suitable in the preparation of baby food, as well as sodium-free diets. Today it belongs to the Danone group.

Composition (mg/l):
Calcium:	9.9	
Magnesium:	6.1	
Sodium:	9.4	
Potassium:	5.7	
Sulphates:	6.9	
Bicarbonates:	65.3	
Chloride:	8.4	
Nitrates:	6.3	
PH:	7	
Mineralization:	109	

Indications:
Suitable for low-sodium diets and baby bottle preparation.
Dominant flavors:
Light and sweet.
Variety:
Still.

WATTWILLER

Mineral Water (Alsace)

Origin: Roman vestiges prove that this water was already known in Antiquity. In 1741, Friedrich Bachers, state physician, declared: "The water of Wattwiller has a soul." It was bottled for the first time in the early 19th century and the Académie de Médecine recognized its virtues in 1850. During the First World War, the village was destroyed, along with the plant, which was only rebuilt in 1924. It resumed operation, but the spring went unused once again between 1972 and 1992. Wattwiller mineral water originates in the heart of the Ballons des Vosges regional natural park. High in sulphates, calcium and fluor (2 mg/l), a little sodic and without a trace of nitrates, it is a diuretic. Its calcium content makes it valuable the growing up period.

Composition (mg/l):
Calcium:	288	
Magnesium:	20.1	
Sodium:	3	
Potassium:	1.4	
Sulphates:	678	
Bicarbonates:	142	
Chloride:	3.9	
Nitrates:	0	
PH:	7.5	
Mineralization:	1.092	

Indications:
Suitable for sodium-free diets and baby bottle preparation.
Dominant flavors:
Neutral smell and taste.
Variety:
Still.

Germany

APOLLINARIS

Mineral Water (Rhineland-Palatinate)

Origin: In the middle of the 19th century, a wine grower named Georg Kreutzberg from the Bad Neuenahr region was worried about the abnormal growth of the vines that he had planted on a hillside. He dug up the soil and noticed that carbonic gas was emanating from it. He dug more deeply and discovered a tumultuous source that gushed forth lukewarm water from the limestone underground (1852). He called it Apollinaris and took it upon himself to sell it. This mineral water, one of the most well-known in Germany today, is exported to several countries. Rich in minerals, it is high in bicarbonates, sodium and magnesium, with a notable calcium content. With added fluor, it contributes to the fight against tooth decay.

Composition (mg/l):

		Indications:
Calcium:	85.4	Not recommended for strict sodium-free diets.
Magnesium.	117	**Dominant flavors:**
Sodium:	415	Fresh and bubbly.
Potassium:	24.4	**Variety:**
Sulphates:	82	Carbonated.
Bicarbonates:	1.708	
Chloride:	101	
Nitrates:	3	
PH:	5.9	
Mineralization:	2.564	

BAD VILBELER URQUELLE

Mineral Water (Hessen)

Origin: Bad Vilbeler Ur-Quelle belongs to the Hassia & Luisen group, whose mineral waters are bottled in the city of Bad Vilbel, near Frankfurt-on-Main. Symbol of the brand, the presumptuous Friedrich Groshola, "Marketing Director" from the last century, is boldly featured on the label. Bad-Vilbeler Ur-Quelle natural mineral water is rich in bicarbonates, calcium and sodium. Its 0.37 mg/l fluor content makes it useful in the prevention of tooth decay.

Composition (mg/l):

		Indications:
Calcium:	174	Not suitable for low-sodium diets or baby bottle preparation.
Magnesium:	25.8	
Sodium:	90	
Potassium:	13.6	**Dominant flavors:**
Sulphates:	36	Mineral flavor.
Bicarbonates:	702	**Variety:**
Chloride:	93.6	Sparkling.
Nitrates:	1.9	
PH:	5.4	
Mineralization:	1.085	

ELISABETHEN

Mineral Water (Hessen)

Origin: Bad Vilbel, in the Hessen region, east of Frankfurt-on-Main, is a city that has long been known for its mineral waters. At one time, it had twenty-two mineral water companies; today that number has been reduced to thirteen. The city is located above a series of fissures that reach as far as the aquiferous layer of the ancient volcanic Vogelsberg mountains. The Elisabethen natural mineral water spring has a fluor content of 0.9 mg/l, which allows it to play a role in the fight against tooth decay. Three versions are available: carbonated, sparkling and "almost still."

Composition (mg/l):

		Indications:
Calcium:	110	Suitable for all diets.
Magnesium:	20.2	**Dominant flavors:**
Sodium:	/	Neutral water.
Potassium:	5.4	**Varieties:**
Sulphates:	43	Carbonated, sparkling and "almost still".
Bicarbonates:	397	
Chloride:	6.3	
Nitrates:	/	
PH:	/	
Mineralization:	/	

FÜRST BISMARCK QUELLE

Mineral Water (Hamburg)

Origin: In operation since 1906, Fürst Bismarck Quelle is the best-selling water in northern Germany, especially in the cities of Hamburg and Berlin. The lands from which it springs formerly belonged to the family of the first German Chancellor, who gave his name to the brand. Low in sodium content (14 mg/l), it is recommended for people restricted to a sodium-free diet.

Composition (mg/l):

		Indications:
Calcium:	79	Suitable for sodium-free diets.
Magnesium:	5.4	
Sodium:	14	**Dominant flavors:**
Potassium:	/	Refreshing.
Sulphates:	53	**Varieties:**
Bicarbonates:	206	Still, sparkling and carbonated.
Chloride:	22	
Nitrates:	/	
PH:	/	
Mineralization:	409	

GEROLSTEINER

Mineral Water (Palatinate)

Origin: Gerolsteiner Sprudel, created in 1888, distributed its water in earthenware jugs before switching to glass in 1900. Its two principal productions are Gerolsteiner Sprudel (naturally carbonated water enriched with carbonic gas) and Gerolsteiner Stille Quelle (partially degasified). The first is the top-selling mineral water in Germany. Water from the Gerolstein spring is rich in mineral salts (2,487 mg/l). Rich in bicarbonates, calcium and magnesium, sodium content is as high as 118 mg/l. The company was the first to adopt, in 1988, a returnable plastic bottle, designed to be re-used ten to fifteen times before being recycled.

Composition (mg/l):

		Indications:
Calcium:	348	Not recommended for low-sodium diets. The richness in bicarbonates of these waters makes them suitable for hepatic ailments.
Magnesium:	108	
Sodium:	118	
Potassium:	10.8	
Sulphates:	36.3	
Bicarbonates:	1.817	**Dominant flavors:**
Chloride:	39.7	Fresh water with a metallic smell.
Nitrates:	5.1	**Varieties:**
PH:	/	Carbonated and sparkling.
Mineralization:	2.487	

GÜSTROWER SCHLOSSQUELL

Mineral Water (Mecklemburg)

Origin: Güstrower Schlossquell water (at the Gustrower castle's spring) has been bottled and sold since 1851. Very low in minerals, very pure (fewer than 0.5 mg/l of nitrates) and with a sodium content of only 16.1 mg/l, this mineral water is therefore suitable for people restricted to a low-sodium diet and infants, even though it is lightly carbonated.

Composition (mg/l):

		Indications:
Calcium:	98.1	Suitable for low-sodium diets and infants.
Magnesium:	12.2	
Sodium:	16.1	**Dominant flavors:**
Potassium:	2.1	Neutral water.
Sulphates:	40.2	**Variety:**
Bicarbonates:	322	Lightly sparkling.
Chloride:	20.1	
Nitrates:	<0.5	
PH:	/	
Mineralization:	/	

HASSIA SPRUDEL

Mineral Water (Hessen)

Origin: The original spring, the oldest in Bad Vilbel, east of Frankfurt-on-Main, was discovered in 1864 by Johann Hinkel (it bubbles up in a small temple in the municipal park). The eponymous water that is sold today is harnessed 330 yd underground in the aquiferous layer stemming from the volcanic Vogelsberg mountains. It is owned by the Hassia & Luisen group, which controls two other springs in the region, Elisabethen, Luisen Brunnen and in Saxony, the Lichtenauer spring. With a moderate mineral content, with bicarbonates, calcium, sodium and a notable magnesium content, it is distributed in carbonated (Hassia Sprudel) and sparkling (Hassia Leicht) versions.

HARZER GRAUHOF

Mineral Water (Lower Saxony)

Origin: This natural mineral water's spring was discovered in 1877 in the northern part of the Harz Forest, southeast of Hanover. Harzer Grauhof is especially widespread in the Hanover, Bremen and Leipzig regions. It belongs to the Blaue Quellen group. It is recommended for people restricted to a low-sodium diet due to its low sodium content (17.7 mg/l). The still version is suitable for infants.

HIRSCHQUELLE

Mineral Water (Black Forest)

Origin: Known for centuries, Hirschquelle mineral water ("the buck's spring") bubbles up naturally carbonated at Bad Teinach in the Black Forest, in an area protected from pollution (1.7 mg/l of nitrates). It is run by Mineralbrunnen Uberkingen-Teinach. With bicarbonates, calcium and sodium, it also contains 1 mg/l of fluor, which makes it especially useful in the prevention of tooth decay. It is not suitable for people suffering from hypertension, nor for those on a low-sodium diet, because it contains 261 mg/l of sodium.

Composition (mg/l):		Indications:
Calcium:	123	Suitable for baby bottle preparation.
Magnesium:	11	
Sodium:	17.7	**Dominant flavors:**
Potassium:	/	Neutral water.
Sulphates:	65	**Varieties:**
Bicarbonates:	329	Still, sparkling and bubbly.
Chloride:	33	
Nitrates:	/	
PH:	/	
Mineralization:	556	

Composition (mg/l):		Indications:
Calcium:	186	Not suitable for low-sodium diets or baby bottle preparation.
Magnesium:	36.1	
Sodium:	228	
Potassium:	26.7	**Dominant flavors:**
Sulphates:	42	Mildly mineral taste.
Bicarbonates:	1,144	**Varieties:**
Chloride:	121	Carbonated and sparkling.
Nitrates:	/	
PH:	/	
Mineralization:	/	

Composition (mg/l):		Indications:
Calcium:	216	Not suitable for sodium-free diets.
Magnesium:	29.2	
Sodium:	261	**Dominant flavors:**
Potassium:	11.6	Light, mildly carbonated.
Sulphates:	85	
Bicarbonates:	1,343	**Variety:**
Chloride:	41.5	Carbonated.
Nitrates:	1.7	
PH:	/	
Mineralization:	/	

LICHTENAUER

Mineral Water (Saxony)

Origin: The Lichtenau spring is located 7.5 miles northwest of Chemnitz. It is tapped at a depth of 153 yd, in the aquiferous layer fed by waters that have run for centuries through the Erzgebirge chain which demarcates the Czech-German border. Although the Hassia & Luisen group only began to sell this water in 1991, its annual production is as high as 170 million bottles, making Lichtenauer one of the most important mineral waters in the former East Germany. Low in minerals, with a sodium content of merely 12 mg/l, it is recommended for people on strict sodium-free diets. It exists in carbonated and sparkling versions.

MARGONWASSER

Mineral Water (Saxony)

Origin: The Margonwasser springs are located in a wooded region of Muglitzal, between the Erzgebirge and the Elbe Valley near Dresden. The first, whose therapeutic qualities were quickly recognized, was discovered at the end of the 19th century by Gottfried Moritz Gossel. Nationalized after 1945, the springs were reprivatized during reunification by the Gerolsteiner Brunnen company, who, after investing in it, brought production levels to 120 million bottles per year. Margonwasser is made from a blend of 12 springs harnessed between 118 and 165 yd underground. It exists in two varieties: Margon Mineralwasser (strongly carbonated) and Margon Medium (moderately carbonated).

NEUSELTERS MINERAL QUELLE

Mineral Water (Hessen)

Origin: This mineral water's spring was discovered in 1887 by the mayor of Selters, Friedrich Wilhelm Neu, who was fascinated by hydrology. He sold the water that bears his name locally and started to bottle it in glass in 1920. Neuselters natural mineral water contains a good balance of calcium, magnesium and sodium. Now it belongs to Blaue Quellen, the second-leading German mineral water company. It is distributed in still, sparkling and carbonated varieties.

Composition (mg/l):		Indications:
Calcium:	56	Suitable for the strictest sodium-free diets.
Magnesium:	9.1	
Sodium:	12	**Dominant flavors:**
Potassium:	1.6	Neutral water.
Sulphates:	52	**Varieties:**
Bicarbonates:	160	Carbonated and sparkling.
Chloride:	15.3	
Nitrates:	/	
PH:	/	
Mineralization:	/	

Composition (mg/l):		Indications:
Calcium:	84	Not suitable for low-sodium diets.
Magnesium:	18	
Sodium:	20	**Dominant flavors:**
Potassium:	1	Neutral water.
Sulphates:	118	**Varieties:**
Bicarbonates:	206	Carbonated and sparkling.
Chloride:	31	
Nitrates:	/	
PH:	/	
Mineralization:	/	

Composition (mg/l):		Indications:
Calcium:	116	Not suitable for very strict sodium-free diets or baby bottle preparation.
Magnesium:	29	
Sodium:	104	
Potassium:	5.5	**Dominant flavors:**
Sulphates:	20	Neutral water.
Bicarbonates:	598	**Varieties:**
Chloride:	120	Still, sparkling and carbonated.
Nitrates:	94.3	
PH:	/	
Mineralization:	994	

PETERSTALER

Mineral Water (Black Forest)

Origin: The Peterstal mineral water springs are located between Strasbourg and Freudenstadt, in the heart of the Black Forest. Already known by Benedictine monks for over 700 years, they were most appreciated for their curative properties in the 16th century. Starting in 1832, they were distributed in earthenware jugs, especially in Strasbourg. The spring of the water sold today, discovered in 1926, is located about 328 yd underground. With bicarbonates, calcium, sodium and sulphates, it is moderately mineralized. With its relatively high fluor content, it can play a role in the prevention of tooth decay. It is distributed in still, carbonated and sparkling varieties.

Composition (mg/l):

Calcium:	216	
Magnesium:	49	
Sodium:	215	
Potassium:	17	
Sulphates:		
Bicarbonates:	1.138	
Chloride:	21	
Nitrates:	/	
PH:	/	
Mineralization:	/	

Indications:
Not suitable for low-sodium diets.
Dominant flavors:
Mineral nuances.
Varieties:
Still, carbonated and sparkling.

RENNSTEIG

Mineral Water (Thuringe)

Origin: The Rennsteig natural mineral water spring, harnessed in Schmalkalden, is run by the Thuringer Waldquell Mineralbrunnen company. It is lightlly mineralized (471 mg/l) and weak in sodium (12.4 mg/l). Rennsteig mineral water, made effervescent by the addition of carbonic gas, is produced in two varieties: Rennsteig Sprudel, sparkling, in green bottles (with a green label) and Rennsteig Medium, less effervescent, in clear bottles (with a blue label). Strangely, the label specifies: "Suitable for the preparation of food for infants", although in France the use of carbonated water for babies is not recommended.

Composition (mg/l):

Calcium:	73.2	
Magnesium:	26.5	
Sodium:	12.4	
Potassium:	3.9	
Sulphates:	141	
Bicarbonates:	186	
Chloride:	15.3	
Nitrates:	/	
PH:	/	
Mineralization:	471	

Indications:
Suitable for strict sodium-free diets.
Dominant flavors:
Lightly salty.
Varieties:
Carbonated and sparkling.

ROSBACHER KLASSISCH

Mineral Water (Hessen)

Origin: Rosbach, 94 miles from Frankfurt-on-Main, is located southwest of the Taunus range and is known for its thermal baths. Its waters were known by the Romans and Germans. The virtues of the Rosbach springs are confirmed by archives dating back to 1584. The springs have been run industrially for a hundred years. The waters rise from the depths as a result of the action of carbonic gas that forms layers that can be reached by drilling down 110 yd. Rosbacher Klassisch is rich in minerals (1.645 mg/l), with bicarbonates, calcium and magnesium. It contains the virtually ideal calcium/magnesium ratio of 2/1. Partially degasified, it is a sparkling water.

Composition (mg/l):

Calcium:	209	
Magnesium:	92.8	
Sodium:	85	
Potassium:	4	
Sulphates:	12	
Bicarbonates:	1.079	
Chloride:	141	
Nitrates:	/	
PH:	/	
Mineralization:	1.645	

Indications:
Not suitable for very strict sodium-free diets.
Dominant flavors:
Mineral smell and taste.
Variety:
Sparkling.

SINZIGER

Mineral Water (Rhineland)

Origin: A spring was discovered in Sinzig in 1853, in the schistose Eifel range. Its mineral water was quickly commercialized and sold in earthenware bottles. In 1857, the thermal spa was named Bad Sinzig. In 1865, Apollinaris bought the bottling rights with a clause allowing it to interrupt its sale for at least thirty years. Shortly thereafter, the spring and spa were closed. Reopened in 1927, a first bottling line was put in place in 1929. The spring was approved by the state in 1933. Rich in mineral salts, Sinziger, with bicarbonates and magnesium, is very pure (0.9 mg/l of nitrates). It is distributed in still and reinforced with carbonic gas versions.

Composition (mg/l):

Calcium:	53.9	
Magnesium:	61	
Sodium:	143	
Potassium:	9.3	
Sulphates:	53	
Bicarbonates:	695	
Chloride:	69.8	
Nitrates:	0.9	
PH:	/	
Mineralization:	1.102	

Indications:
Not suitable for low-sodium diets or baby bottle preparation.
Dominant flavors:
Freshness and sweetness.
Varieties:
Still and carbonated.

THÜRINGER WALDQUELL

Mineral Water (Thuringe)

Origin: The historic city of Schmalkalde is located on the southern slope of the Thuringe Forest. It was there that the Schmalkalde League was formed between the princes and the Protestant German cities in 1531, which then allied itself with François I to protect the Lutheran Church from Emperor Charles V. Thuringer Waldquell is harnessed 1.25 miles from the city, by an artesian well 88 yd in depth. Lightly mineralized, with magnesium and low in sodium (28.4 mg/l), it has carbonic gas added to it before being bottled in a factory 547 yd away. Two varieties are sold, a carbonated water and a sparkling one labelled "Medium". The annual factory production is greater than one million hl.

Composition (mg/l):

Calcium:	106	
Magnesium:	50	
Sodium:	28.4	
Potassium:	2.9	
Sulphates:	241	
Bicarbonates:	281	
Chloride:	39.4	
Nitrates:	/	
PH:	/	
Mineralization:	/	

Indications:
Suitable for all diets.
Dominant flavors:
Neutral water.
Varieties:
Carbonated and sparkling.

ÜBERKINGER

Mineral Water (Baden-Wurtemberg)

Origin: Uberkinger natural mineral water has been known since the Middle Ages. At the time, the hot water springs of Baden-Wurtemberg were already well-known. In 1750, this water was sold locally in earthenware jars. In 1850, it began to be packaged in bottles. Uberkinger has only really been distributed in southern Germany and more specifically, in the prosperous triangle of Stuttgart, Munich and Nuremburg, since 1950.

Composition (mg/l):

Calcium:	20	
Magnesium:	15.8	
Sodium:	1.090	
Potassium:	17.8	
Sulphates:	1.110	
Bicarbonates:	1.480	
Chloride:	100	
Nitrates:	< 0.1	
PH:	/	
Mineralization:	/	

Indications:
Suitable for all diets.
Dominant flavors:
Slightly bitter.
Varieties:
Carbonated and sparkling.

Italy

ACQUACHIARA

Mineral Water (Venetia)

Origin: Nuova Acquachiara is a natural mineral water harnessed in Valli del Pasubio, in the province of Venetia. Weak in minerals (141.8 mg/l), with a low sodium content (1.4 mg/l), Nuova Acquachiara, which possesses diuretic properties, can be drunk without restriction. In 1992, Acquachiara was officially recognized as an oligo-mineral water.

Composition (mg/l):		Indications:
Calcium:	29	Suitable for all diets.
Magnesium:	16.2	Diuretic effects. Suitable
Sodium:	1.4	for low-sodium diets.
Potassium:	0.6	**Dominant flavors:**
Sulphates:	10	Neutral water.
Bicarbonates:	156.2	**Variety:**
Chloride:	1.7	Still.
Nitrates:	4.4	
PH:	8	
Mineralization:	141.8	

COURMAYEUR

Mineral Water (Val d'Aoste)

Origin: Significant archaeological ruins prove that there was a mineral bath spa in Courmayer in the Val d'Aoste during the Roman era. Writings from the 17th century attest to the fact that these waters were used as a form of drink therapy. The spring emerges at the foot of Mount Blanc, at an elevation of 1,338 yd, in an area protected from all industry and agriculture-related pollution. Courmayer water, rich in minerals (2,264 mg/l), is high in calcium, magnesium and sulphates. Its low sodium content (1 mg/l) makes it ideal for the strictest sodium-free diets. Its distribution in France is planned for the second trimester of 2000.

Composition (mg/l):		Indications:
Calcium:	517	Suitable for the strictest
Magnesium:	67	sodium-free diets.
Sodium:	1	Not suitable for baby
Potassium:	2	bottle preparation.
Sulphates:	1,371	**Dominant flavors:**
Bicarbonates:	168	Mildly alkaline.
Chloride:	<1	**Variety:**
Nitrates:	<2	Still.
PH:	7.4	
Mineralization:	2,264	

DAGGIO

Mineral Water (Lombardy)

Origin: Daggio natural mineral water is harnessed at a temperature of 49 °F at the Introbio spring in Primaluna, near Lecco, in the Lombardy province of Como. It is run by the Norda company, which also owns the Ducale spring in Emilia-Romagna. With 44.5 g/l of dry extract, Daggio is a very poorly mineralized water, undoubtedly one of the least mineralized of all Italian mineral waters. Thanks to its particularly low sodium content 1.5 mg/l, it is ideal for people restricted to even the most strict sodium-free diet. It also has diuretic properties.

Composition (mg/l):		Indications:
Calcium:	7.9	Suitable for strict
Magnesium:	2.0	sodium-free diets
Sodium:	1.5	and baby bottle preparation.
Potassium:	0.5	**Dominant flavors:**
Sulphates:	4.5	Neutral water.
Bicarbonates:	/	**Variety:**
Chloride:	0.6	Still.
Nitrates:	2.7	
PH:	7.5	
Mineralization:	/	

DUCALE

Mineral Water (Emilia-Romagna)

Origin: Ducale natural mineral water emerges at a temperature of 48.5 °F from a spring located in Tortogno, in the Parma province of Emilia-Romagna. Like Daggio, a Lombardy mineral water spring owned by the same company (Norda), it is a diuretic. Remarkably low in sodium (1.6 mg/l), it is suitable for people suffering from hypertension or restricted to a very strict sodium-free diet.

Composition (mg/l):		Indications:
Calcium:	12.6	Suitable for the strictest
Magnesium:	2.1	sodium-free diets,
Sodium:	1.6	baby bottle preparation,
Potassium:	0.5	and people suffering
Sulphates:	7.4	from hypertension.
Bicarbonates:	/	**Dominant flavors:**
Chloride:	3.8	Neutral water.
Nitrates:	2	**Variety:**
PH:	7.8	Still.
Mineralization:	/	

EUREKA

Mineral Water (Pouilles)

Origin: Eureka natural mineral water is tapped at the Madonnina spring, located in Cornigliano d'Otrante, in the Lecce province (Pouilles). Low in minerals (395 mg/l), it contains a fairly significant amount of magnesium (29 mg/l). Its sodium content (33.4 mg/l) is a bit too high for strict sodium-free diets and in the preparation of infant food. Its production level attains 100,000 bottles per hour.

Composition (mg/l):		Indications:
Calcium:	61.5	Not suitable for
Magnesium:	29	sodium-free diets or baby
Sodium:	33.4	bottle preparation.
Potassium:	3.6	**Dominant flavors:**
Sulphates:	11.8	Neutral water.
Bicarbonates:	316.6	**Variety:**
Chloride:	58.5	Still.
Nitrates:	12	
PH:	7.3	
Mineralization:	395	

FERRARELLE

Mineral Water (Campania)

Origin: Ferrarelle mineral water has its source in the Riardo volcanic basin, north-east of Naples. Recognized since Antiquity as a high quality water for its therapeutic virtues, Ferrarelle began to expand in 1783 and today is one of the most popular sparkling waters in Italy.

Composition (mg/l):		Indications:
Calcium:	408	Suitable for all diets.
Magnesium:	23	**Dominant flavors:**
Sodium:	50	Neutral water.
Potassium:	41	**Variety:**
Sulphates:	5	Sparkling.
Bicarbonates:	1,513	
Chloride:	21	
Nitrates:	4	
PH:	/	
Mineralization:	/	

FIUGGI
Mineral Water (Latium)

Origin: Fiuggi Fonte is a mineral bath spa east of Rome, located at an elevation of 678 yd on a hillside surrounded by forests. Its waters, used for the treatment of kidney, bladder and urinary ailments, have been known since the era of Pope Boniface VIII (who died in 1303). The first illustrious person who returned to health thanks to the Fiuggi waters, around 1500, was Michelangelo Buonarroti. Fiuggi natural mineral water, poor in minerals, is high in bicarbonates, calcium, magnesium and chloride. A diuretic, it facilitates in the elimination of toxins, is useful for the treatment of renal problems and is recommended for its depurative quality.

Composition (mg/l):		Indications:
Calcium:	15.9	Not suitable for low-sodium diets or baby bottle preparation.
Magnesium:	6.3	
Sodium:	6.4	
Potassium:	4.4	**Dominant flavors:**
Sulphates:	6	Neutral water.
Bicarbonates:	81.7	**Varieties:**
Chloride:	13.9	Still and carbonated.
Nitrates:	7	
PH:	6.8	
Mineralization:	122	

LEVISSIMA
Mineral Water (Lombardy)

Origin: A poorly mineralized water, Levissima's spring is located at an elevation of 2,012 yd in the Italian Alps. A pure water with a low sodium content (1.7 mg/l), it was officially recognized as a mineral water in 1965. It is available in still and carbonated versions.

Composition (mg/l):		Indications:
Calcium:	19.8	Suitable for baby bottle preparation.
Magnesium:	1.8	
Sodium:	1.7	**Dominant flavors:**
Potassium:	1.8	Neutral water.
Sulphates:	14.2	**Varieties:**
Bicarbonates:	56.5	Still and carbonated.
Chloride:	0.3	
Nitrates:	1.5	
PH:	7.8	
Mineralization:	73.5	

PANNA
Mineral Water (Tuscany)

Origin: Panna mineral water emerges in the Apennines of Tuscany, at an altitude of 1,230 yd on an estate that once belonged to the Medici family, at the heart of a wild natural reserve known for its abundance of wildlife—the Medicis acquired the Panna spring in the 14th century. Poor in minerals (144 mg/l), Panna, with a low sodium content, is recommended for people on a low-sodium diet and suitable in the preparation of food for infants.

Composition (mg/l):		Indications:
Calcium:	32.8	Suitable for low-sodium diets and baby bottle preparation.
Magnesium:	6.6	
Sodium:	6.2	
Potassium:	0.9	**Dominant flavors:**
Sulphates:	24.5	Sweet flavor.
Bicarbonates:	103	**Variety:**
Chloride:	7.6	Still.
Nitrates:	3.7	
PH:	7.8	
Mineralization:	144	

ROCCHETTA
Mineral Water (Umbria)

Origin: At the beginning of the 13th century, Pope Innocent III and the young Frederick of Hohenstaufen, King of Sicily and future German emperor (whom the pope was educating), liked to stroll together in Umbria and used to quench their thirst at a spring known since Antiquity. It is from that very spring that Rocchetta mineral water emerges, above the Rocca Flea that dominates Gualdo Tadino in the Perugia province, a small picturesque city at an elevation of 585 yd. On the market since 1903, Rocchetta, poorly mineralized (176 mg/l) and low in sodium (4.6 mg/l), is recommended for low-sodium diets. A diuretic, it aids urinary excretion. The carbonated version is labelled "Brio Blu".

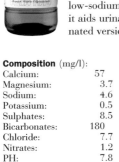

Composition (mg/l):		Indications:
Calcium:	57	Suitable for low-sodium diets and baby bottle preparation.
Magnesium:	3.7	
Sodium:	4.6	
Potassium:	0.5	**Dominant flavors:**
Sulphates:	8.5	Neutral water.
Bicarbonates:	180	**Varieties:**
Chloride:	7.7	Still and carbonated.
Nitrates:	1.2	
PH:	7.8	
Mineralization:	176	

SAN BENEDETTO
Mineral Water (Venetia)

Origin: *"L'acqua della salute San Benedetto"* was already known at the time of the Republic of Venice. Wealthy Venetian families who enjoyed its curative virtues had it transported from the spring, located a little over 19 miles from the Dolomites. The water coming from the snowmelt seeps slowly into the rocky mountain soil and gradually acquires its mineralization over the course of its descent to a depth of 219 yd. It emerges naturally, in a protected area (6.6 mg/l of nitrates) at a temperature of 59 °F—which is why San Benedetto is nicknamed the "water of springtime". Poorly mineralized, it is low in sodium (6.8 mg/l), but has a notable magnesium content (28 mg/l).

Composition (mg/l):		Indications:
Calcium:	46	Diuretic properties, facilitates digestion.
Magnesium:	28	
Sodium:	6.8	**Dominant flavors:**
Potassium:	1	Neutral water.
Sulphates:	5.8	**Variety:**
Bicarbonates:	287	Still.
Chloride:	2.4	
Nitrates:	/	
PH:	7.7	
Mineralization:	251	

SAN BERNARDO
Mineral Water (Alps)

Origin: Discovered over a century ago in the Italian Alps near the San-Bernardo pass, at an elevation of 1,093 yd, San Bernardo water emerges at 41-43 °F. Amid the enthusiasts of this natural mineral water were Napoleon I, as well as King Victor Emmanuel. In 1926, a royal decree authorized its bottling for the first time. Very poorly mineralized, San Bernardo has diuretic properties. It is distributed in still, sparkling and carbonated versions.

Composition (mg/l):		Indications:
Calcium:	11,5	Suitable for baby bottle preparation.
Magnesium:	0,5	
Sodium:	0,5	**Dominant flavors:**
Potassium:	0,4	Light taste.
Sulphates:	2	**Varieties:**
Bicarbonates:	35	Still, sparkling and carbonated.
Chloride:	0,6	
Nitrates:	1,3	
PH:	7,3	
Mineralization:	39	

SAN PELLEGRINO

Mineral Water (Lombardy)

Origin: San Pellegrino's spring is situated in the grandiose location of the Brembana Valley near Bergamo. Already frequented by the Romans, the spring was discovered in the thirteenth century by San Pellegrino, a monk pilgrim who gave it his name and his emblem—the pilgrim's star. Reinforced by natural carbonic gas, moderately mineralized, rich in bicarbonates, calcium and magnesium, moderately chloridated and sodic, it is a diuretic and very pure (less than 1 mg/l of nitrates). Due to its sodium content (42 mg/l), it is not recommended for people on a sodium-free diet. Bottled for the first time in 1899, San Pellegrino is part of the Perrier-Vittel group (Nestlé).

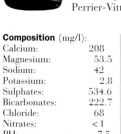

Composition (mg/l):		Indications:
Calcium:	208	Not suitable for
Magnesium:	53.5	sodium-free diets.
Sodium:	42	**Dominant flavors:**
Potassium:	2.8	Mildly sparkling.
Sulphates:	534.6	**Variety:**
Bicarbonates:	222.7	Sparkling.
Chloride:	68	
Nitrates:	< 1	
PH:	7.5	
Mineralization:	1,074	

SANCARLO SPINONE

Mineral Water (Lombardy)

Origin: Sancarlo Spinone natural mineral water emerges from the Fonte Nuova spring in Spinone al Lago in the Lombardy province of Bergamo. It came on the market in 1948. The installations were expanded in 1952, the era when the bottling line was created. The limited company Fonti Sancarlo, founded in 1953, proceeded its sale on a bigger scale. Sancarlo Spinone, registered as an oligo-mineral water, weakly mineralized (410.4 mg/l), moderately rich in bicarbonates, calcium, and magnesium and little sodic (6 mg/l), is recognized for its diuretic properties. It exists in still, sparkling, and carbonated versions.

Composition (mg/l):		Indications:
Calcium:	100.8	Suitable for low-sodium
Magnesium:	27.2	diets and baby bottle
Sodium:	6	preparation.
Potassium:	0.8	**Dominant flavors:**
Sulphates:	66.6	Neutral water.
Bicarbonates:	360	**Varieties:**
Chloride:	4.1	Still, sparkling
Nitrates:	5.4	and carbonated.
PH:	7.4	
Mineralization:	410.4	

SANTA CLARA

Mineral Water (Liguria)

Origin: anta Clara natural mineral water spring is located in the Ligurian Apennines, at an elevation of 897 yd, in the Borzonasca community (Genoa province). Poorly mineralized (125 mg/l), Santa Clara benefits from the fact that it is registered as an oligo-mineral water. A diuretic, it favors the elimination of urinary acid and stimulates digestion. With a very poor sodium content (3.5 mg/l), it is recommended for people restricted to a low-sodium diet.

Composition (mg/l):		Indications:
Calcium:	36	Suitable for low-sodium
Magnesium:	4.8	diets and baby bottle
Sodium:	3.5	preparation.
Potassium:	0.3	**Dominant flavors:**
Sulphates:	11.6	Neutral water.
Bicarbonates:	117.6	**Variety:**
Chloride:	3.5	Still.
Nitrates:	2.5	
PH:	7.6	
Mineralization:	125	

ULIVETO

Mineral Water (Tuscany)

Origin: The Tuscan Uliveto mineral bath spa is located on a picturesque hillside covered with olive trees near Pisa. In the twelfth century, according to the legend, Frederick I of Barbarossa's army, marching toward Bientina, halted at Vicopisano where the soldiers quenched their thirst with the local water. Antonio Muratori (1672-1750) mentioned its curative virtues in one of his chronicles. Dr. Giuli then attested to its therapeutic value. A company was established in 1910 to sell it in bottles. Rich in mineral salts, Uliveto is rich in bicarbonates, calcium and sodium with a remarkable magnesium and potassium content. It is recommended for the treatment of digestive ailments.

Composition (mg/l):		Indications:
Calcium:	202	Not suitable for
Magnesium:	29.8	low-sodium diets.
Sodium:	113.7	**Dominant flavors:**
Potassium:	11.6	Mildly effervescent
Sulphates:	151	and salty.
Bicarbonates:	683.2	**Variety:**
Chloride:	121.4	Sparkling.
Nitrates:	5.9	
PH:	/	
Mineralization:	/	

VERA

Mineral Water

(Trentin-Haut-Adige)

Origin: Already known in Roman Antiquity, this light and poorly mineralized water (160 mg/l) has its spring in the Dolomites. Operated industrially since 1979, it rapidly became one of the most well-known mineral waters in Italy. With a very low sodium content (2 mg/l), it is suitable for people restricted to a sodium-free diet and in the preparation of food for infants. Vera mineral water, run by Perrier-Vittel (Nestlé), is available in still, sparkling and carbonated versions.

Composition (mg/l):		Indications:
Calcium:	36	Suitable for
Magnesium:	13	sodium-free diets and baby
Sodium:	2	bottle preparation.
Potassium:	0.6	**Dominant flavors:**
Sulphates:	18	Mildly alkaline
Bicarbonates:	154	taste with a rocky nuance.
Chloride:	2.1	**Varieties:**
Nitrates:	3.6	Still, sparkling
PH:	8	and carbonated.
Mineralization:	160	

Portugal

ÁGUA DE LUSO

Mineral Water (Central-West)

Origin: Agua de Luso natural mineral water emerges at the Luso mineral bath spa, established in the eighteenth century. Known for 150 years for its therapeutic properties, this is the most widely distributed water in Portugal since the construction of a high-volume bottling plant (annual production of 170 million liters). Very poorly mineralized (under 50 mg/l), low in sodium and harnessed in a protected area, it is very pure and has a negligible nitrate content. A diuretic, it is recommended in the fight against urinary ailments. Agua de Luso is distributed in bottles, but also recently became available in the form of ice cubes as well.

AGUA CASTELLO

Mineral Water (South-East)

Origin: Agua Castello naturally carbonated mineral water from south-eastern Portugal has been in operation since 1899. This strongly gaseous hundred year-old brand is one of the most popular waters in the country. A poorly mineralized water (50 mg/l), Agua Castello belongs today to the Perrier-Vittel group (Nestlé).

CAMPILHO

Mineral Water (North)

Origin: Campilho naturally gaseous mineral water has its spring in the Alto Duro mountains in the northern part of Portugal. The commercial operation of the spring began over a century ago, with a distribution devoted primarily to the north of the country. Today, Campilho belongs to the Perrier-Vittel group (Nestlé).

Composition (mg/l):		Indications:
Calcium:	101	Suitable for all diets.
Magnesium:	30.6	**Dominant flavors:**
Sodium:	39.5	Strongly gaseous,
Potassium:	0.8	very refreshing.
Sulphates:	20	**Variety:**
Bicarbonates:	373	Carbonated.
Chloride:	83	
Nitrates:	/	
PH:	7.1	
Mineralization:	501	

Composition (mg/l):		Indications:
Calcium:	0.6	Not suitable for strict
Magnesium:	1.6	sodium-free diets or
Sodium:	6.1	baby bottle preparation.
Potassium:	0.7	**Dominant flavors:**
Sulphates:	1.4	Neutral water.
Bicarbonates:	8.4	**Variety:**
Chloride:	9	Still.
Nitrates:	1.9	
PH:	5.5	
Mineralization:	42.2	

Composition (mg/l):		Indications:
Calcium:	41.5	Valuable organoleptic
Magnesium:	10.9	properties.
Sodium:	514	**Dominant flavors:**
Potassium:	32	Very mildly
Sulphates:	/	carbonated, light taste.
Bicarbonates:	1,475.5	**Variety:**
Chloride:	26.9	Carbonated.
Nitrates:	1	
PH:	5.9	
Mineralization:	1,576	

PEDRAS SALGADAS

Mineral Water (North-East)

Origin: Pedras Salgadas waters, which emerge in north eastern Portugal, were already known during Roman Antiquity. A mineral bath spa was opened in 1871, but distribution in bottles only began in 1893. Water from the Pedras Salgadas spring is filtered and acquires its mineralization during its run over the course of several years through the many layers of granite rocks. High in minerals (2,735 mg/l +/- 100 mg/l), bicarbonates and calcium, and naturally gaseous, it aids difficult digestion. The Empresa de Engarrafamento de Aguas company, in Amadora, also sells other carbonated waters (Salus Vidago and Melaco) and still waters (Sete Fontes, Caramulo and Ladeira de Envendos).

FASTIO

Mineral Water (Geres)

Origin: Fastio natural mineral water appeared on the Portuguese market in 1979. It is extracted from a cave located in the Serro do Geres granite mountains, in northern Portugal. Fastio is today among the four most popular Portuguese waters. A portion of their production is devoted to exportation, primarily to the United States.

Composition (mg/l):		Indications:
Calcium:	1.4	Suitable for baby
Magnesium:	/	bottle preparation.
Sodium:	4.5	**Dominant flavors:**
Potassium:	0.6	Pure and cristalline water,
Sulphates:	0.5	particularly light taste.
Bicarbonates:	8.9	**Variety:**
Chloride:	4.7	Still.
Nitrates:	/	
PH:	5.7	
Mineralization:	31.9	

Composition (mg/l):		Indications:
Calcium:	160	Aids digestion.
Magnesium:	23.8	**Dominant flavors:**
Sodium:	/	Strong bubbles,
Potassium:	26	salty edge.
Sulphates:	10.5	**Variety:**
Bicarbonates:	1,915	Carbonated.
Chloride:	35	
Nitrates:	/	
PH:	6.1	
Mineralization:	2,735	

Spain

AGUA DE MONDARIZ

Mineral Water (Galicia)

Origin: The virtues of Mondariz water, which emerges near Pontevedra, have been known since Roman times. For centuries, it was used for medicinal baths. In 1873, the spring was officially approved by the state. In 1878, it began to be bottled so that the thermal cure could be expanded beyond the spa itself. At that time, it was sold in pharmacies. The mineral water industry suffered a great deal from the Civil War and did not begin to prosper again until the 1960s. After a fusion between Agua de Mondariz and Fuente del Val in 1972, the company joined the powerful Vichy Catalan group in 1994.

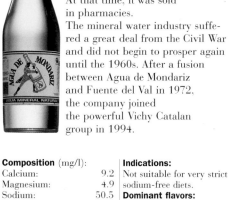

Composition (mg/l):		Indications:
Calcium:	9.2	Not suitable for very strict
Magnesium:	4.9	sodium-free diets.
Sodium:	50.5	**Dominant flavors:**
Potassium:	5.1	Neutral water.
Sulphates:	1.5	**Variety:**
Bicarbonates:	163.4	Still.
Chloride:	17.9	
Nitrates:	1.9	
PH:	6.5	
Mineralization:	181	

FIRGAS LA IDEAL II

Mineral Water (Canary Islands)

Origin: This spring was discovered at the end of the 15th century on the site of the small village of Firgas (Gran Canaria) by the Spanish who had just seized the archipelago (1477). We know that the natives already appreciated its curative virtues. The company that began to sell it, Aguas Minerales de Firgas, was founded in 1930. With its Ideal II spring water (carbonated), whose mineralization is as high as 614 mg/l, it is today the leader in spring water production (it also sells a mineral water labelled Ideal I).

Composition (mg/l):		Indications:
Calcium:	59.3	Not suitable for baby
Magnesium:	32.6	bottle preparation.
Sodium:	40.9	**Dominant flavors:**
Potassium:	2.5	Lightly mineral aftertaste.
Sulphates:	7.8	**Variety:**
Bicarbonates:	403.2	Carbonated.
Chloride:	23.9	
Nitrates:	16.3	
PH:	5.8	
Mineralization:	614	

FONT D'OR

Mineral Water (Catalonia)

Origin: The Font d'Or waterfall (1,093 yd in elevation) emerges in a forest of cork oaks in the Montseny mountain range, near Sant-Hilari-Sacalm, nicknamed the "city of a hundred fountains". The authorization to exploit it was granted in 1956 and production began in 1957. The choice of Font d'Or as the official mineral water of the twenty-fifth Olympic Games (Barcelona, 1992) did a great deal for its reputation. The business acquired an industrial dimension starting in 1986, when it was absorbed by the Vichy Catalan group and an ultra-modern bottling plant was installed. Considered to be a medicinal natural mineral water, it is low in minerals and has diuretic properties.

Composition (mg/l):		Indications:
Calcium:	24	Suitable for sodium-free
Magnesium:	3.9	diets and baby bottle
Sodium:	8.3	preparation.
Potassium:	1.6	**Dominant flavors:**
Sulphates:	14.8	Neutral water.
Bicarbonates:	62.2	**Variety:**
Chloride:	4.6	Still.
Nitrates:	20.9	
PH:	8.2	
Mineralization:	120	

FONT VELLA

Mineral Water (Catalonia)

Origin: Font Vella mineral water, celebrated in 1899 by the Catalan poet Mosen Jacinto Verdaguer Santalo, emerges near Sant-Hilari-Sacalm in the Gerona province. The spring is at an elevation of 908 yd in the Guilleries mountains, in a protected forested area. Rainwater seeps slowly into the fissures of the granite rocks. There it is filtered and acquires its mineralization, emerging more than thirty years later. Weakly mineralized, it is diuretic and not very sodic. It was initially taken from the spring in ceramic jugs, then distributed in carboys. Next came glass bottles, followed in 1958 by plastic bottles. Font Vella is part of the Danone Group.

Composition (mg/l):		Indications:
Calcium:	34.5	Suitable for all diets.
Magnesium:	5.4	**Dominant flavors:**
Sodium:	41.7	Neutral water.
Potassium:	0.8	**Variety:**
Sulphates:	9.8	Still.
Bicarbonates:	212.8	
Chloride:	12.3	
Nitrates:	0	
PH:	7.74	
Mineralization:	251	

FONT SELVA

Mineral Water (Catalonia)

Origin: The Font Selva natural mineral water spring, located near Sant-Hilari-Sacalm in the Gerona province, was discovered in the Guilleries mountains, in one of the largest forested areas in Catalonia. It was officially approved by the state in 1992. Filtered and mineralized by its course through the granite rocks, Font Selva is harnessed 295 yd underground in a protected area (its nitrate content is non-existent). Lightly sulphated and chlorinated, fairly rich in silicates (22.7 mg/l), its fluor content (1.9 mg/l) helps it contribute in the prevention of tooth decay. Like many Spanish mineral waters, it is not only distributed in bottles, but also in big cans.

Composition (mg/l):		Indications:
Calcium:	34.5	Not suitable for very strict
Magnesium:	5.4	sodium-free diets.
Sodium:	41.7	**Dominant flavors:**
Potassium:	0.8	Well-balanced neutral water.
Sulphates:	9.8	**Variety:**
Bicarbonates:	212.8	Still.
Chloride:	12.3	
Nitrates:	0	
PH:	7.74	
Mineralization:	251	

FONTEMILLA

Mineral Water (Sierra de Guadalajara)

Origin: After running for ten to twenty years along calcareous rocks, the Fontemila spring emerges from a rock face in the valley of Mount Culamilla. It was already known during Antiquity because it was close to the route linking Complutum to Caesar Augustae, Roman cities. Water from Culamilla was mentioned in the thirteenth century in King Alphonse XI of Castille's Libro de Monteria ("Hunting Book"). The right to sell it in bottles was granted in 1988. Recognized as a natural mineral water of benefit to the country, it is weakly mineralized, diuretic and useful for the treatment of urinary tracts and the digestive system.

Composition (mg/l):		Indications:
Calcium:	75.2	Suitable for all diets.
Magnesium:	22	**Dominant flavors:**
Sodium:	3.6	Neutral water.
Potassium:	1	**Varieties:**
Sulphates:	19.8	Still and carbonated.
Bicarbonates:	311.8	
Chloride:	8.1	
Nitrates:	4.5	
PH:	7.5	
Mineralization:	/	

FUENSANTA
Mineral Water (Asturias)

Origin: Fuensanta natural mineral water emerges in the Asturias, at the foot of the Picos de Europa, where the Sierra de Pena Mayor rises up, in an impressive geological paradise that is today a natural reserve. Known since the days of Imperial Rome, Fuensanta was recognized by royal decree as a minero-medecinal water of benefit to the country in 1846, due to its balanced composition and therapeutic properties. Harnessed in a protected area, this weakly-mineralized water (265 mg/l) that is low in sodium is recommended for people limited to a rigorous sodium-free diet. Its significant fluor content (1.1 mg/l) allows it to play a useful role in the prevention of tooth decay.

Composition (mg/l):		Indications:
Calcium:	63.3	Suitable for strict
Magnesium:	8.3	sodium free diets
Sodium:	9.9	and baby bottle preparation.
Potassium:	2.5	**Dominant flavors:**
Sulphates:	38.4	Neutral water.
Bicarbonates:	198.3	**Variety:**
Chloride:	8.3	Still.
Nitrates:	/	
PH:	7	
Mineralization:	265	

LANJARÓN
Mineral Water (Andalucia)

Origin: The eternal snows of the Sierra Nevada—called Saluyr ("mountain of sun and snow") by the Arabs—are at the origin of this water that emerges at the Lanjaron spring after being filtered and mineralized over the course of its slow run down the rocks. It is located in the Alegria Valley, in the heart of a natural park that Unesco has classed as a biospheric reserve. According to the legend, it is a miraculous spring with the power to give eternal youth. Sanctioned as a medicinal mineral water in 1818, Lanjaron, weak in minerals, is diuretic. With a sodium content of merely 6 mg/l, it is recommended for very strict sodium-free diets. The company is part of the Danone group.

Composition (mg/l):		Indications:
Calcium:	38.1	Suitable for all diets,
Magnesium:	11.1	including very strict
Sodium:	6.8	sodium-free diets.
Potassium:	/	**Dominant flavors:**
Sulphates:	25.9	Neutral water.
Bicarbonates:	145.8	**Variety:**
Chloride:	3.9	Still.
Nitrates:	/	
PH:	/	
Mineralization:	188	

LES CREUS
Mineral Water (Catalonia)

Origin: The small village of Macanet de Cabrenys where, according to legend, Roland was supposed to have raised a metal barrier against the Saracens, is located in a small valley where springs of the utmost purity, originating in the snows of the Pyrenees, are numerous. It was the village doctor, Jaume Riuro, who was the first to analyze the Creus water after the Civil War, but it was only officially recognized as a medicinal mineral water in 1955. Production was initially performed by hand, but after the formation of the SA Aguas Les Creus in 1968, raised to an industrial level in the seventies. The company has been part of the Vichy Catalan group since 1987. Most of the production is destined for restaurants, cafes and bars.

Composition (mg/l):		Indications:
Calcium:	28	Not suitable for sodium-
Magnesium:	7.3	free diets and baby bottle
Sodium:	11.7	preparation.
Potassium:	1	**Dominant flavors:**
Sulphates:	12.3	Light water without
Bicarbonates:	119	any dominant
Chloride:	7.2	flavors.
Nitrates:	0	**Variety:**
PH:	7	Still.
Mineralization:	160	

MALAVELLA
Mineral Water (Catalonia)

Origin: The Malavella spring, located in a region of Catalonia known for its medicinal waters, was discovered in 1829 during a preliminary geological study concerning the drilling of a mine that was going to pollute land used for cultivation. Its water, until that time reserved exclusively for mineral baths, only came on the market in 1940. Vichy Catalan, a shareholder since 1979, absorbed the company that operated it in 1986. Rich in minerals (3,049 mg/l), bicarbonates, sodium and chloride, with a fluor content of 7.7 mg/l, Malavella water bubbles up at a temperature of 136.5 °F, but it is preferable to drink it cold, after it has been bottled. It is attributed with the property of soothing hangovers.

Composition (mg/l):		Indications:
Calcium:	53.7	Not suitable for sodium-
Magnesium:	9.2	free diets or baby bottle
Sodium:	1,113	preparation.
Potassium:	48	**Dominant flavors:**
Sulphates:	47.3	Pleasantly sparkling water
Bicarbonates:	2,136	on the tongue and in taste.
Chloride:	594.2	**Variety:**
Nitrates:	0	Sparkling.
PH:	6.92	
Mineralization:	3,049	

SOLARES
Mineral Water (Cantabria)

Origin: Known for many years, Solares natural mineral water was officially approved by the state in 1828. It was also awarded a medal of honor in Rotterdam in 1909. A diuretic, it helps digestion. It is distributed in still and carbonated varieties.

Composition (mg/l):		Indications:
Calcium:	73.3	Suitable for all diets.
Magnesium:	25.6	**Dominant flavors:**
Sodium:	87.6	Fluid, almost
Potassium:	1.8	neutral, with a light
Sulphates:	36	aftertaste.
Bicarbonates:	251.9	**Varieties:**
Chloride:	139.5	Still and carbonated.
Nitrates:	/	
PH:	/	
Mineralization:	489	

VICHY CATALÁN
Mineral Water (Catalonia)

Origin: After the discovery of Roman mineral bath ruins in Caldes de Malavella, the doctor Furest I Roca, who was interested in hydrotherapy, acquired the lands and the carbonated water springs that emerge at 140 °F. They were officially approved by the state in 1883 and bottled under the name Vichy Catalan in 1889. A mineral bath spa was inaugurated in 1904. After the interruption of the Civil War, the company resumed its activities, acquired other springs in Catalonia and elsewhere and took on an important role (annual production of 350 million liters of mineral water). Vichy Catalan is rich in minerals, bicarbonates, sodium and chloride, with a fluor content of 7.3 mg/l.

Composition (mg/l):		Indications:
Calcium:	54.1	Not suitable for sodium-
Magnesium:	9.2	free diets or baby bottle
Sodium:	1,110	preparation.
Potassium:	48	**Dominant flavors:**
Sulphates:	47.3	Mildly salty
Bicarbonates:	2,135	and carbonated.
Chloride:	601.5	**Variety:**
Nitrates:	0	Carbonated.
PH:	6.82	
Mineralization:	3,052	

Switzerland

ALPENROSE
Mineral Water (Berne)

Origin: Alpenrose natural mineral water emerges in the Swiss Alps, sheltered from all pollution, at an elevation of 1,640 yd, at a place where a plant called Alpenrose ("rhododendron" in English) blooms. It originates in the highest glaciers of the Bernese Oberland and is enriched with minerals during its slow subterranean descent among the rocky fissures. Rich in minerals (2,200 mg/l), bicarbonates, calcium and sulphates, it has a fairly significant magnesium content (37 mg/l). Alpenrose, packaged exclusively in glass bottles, is distributed in still and sparkling versions.

Composition (mg/l):		Indications:
Calcium:	569	Suitable for low-sodium diets; not suitable for baby bottle preparation.
Magnesium:	37	
Sodium:	5.4	
Potassium:	/	**Dominant flavors:**
Sulphates:	1,290	Rocky taste.
Bicarbonates:	281	**Varieties:**
Chloride:	4.9	Still and sparkling.
Nitrates:	1.6	
PH:	/	
Mineralization:	2,200	

ADELBODNER
Mineral Water (Berne)

Origin: The Adelbodner natural mineral water spring, known since 1509, is one of the highest in Europe. It emerges in the Swiss Alps, far from any pollution, at an elevation of 1,640 yd, in the magnificent Bernese Oberland region. Originating in glaciers, it acquires its mineralization during its slow infiltration of the rock fissures. Belonging to those mineral waters rich in bicarbonates, calcium and sulphates, it has a significant magnesium content (34.5 mg/l), but is low in sodium. It is mildly carbonated before bottling. The spring is operated by the Adelbodner Mineral und Heilquellen company in Adelboden.

Composition (mg/l):		Indications:
Calcium:	537	Not suitable for baby bottle preparation.
Magnesium:	34.5	
Sodium:	/	**Dominant flavors:**
Potassium:	/	Mineral taste.
Sulphates:	1,291	**Variety:**
Bicarbonates:	285	Mildly sparkling.
Chloride:	4.6	
Nitrates:	2.7	
PH:	6.95	
Mineralization:	/	

ARKINA
Mineral Water (Vaud)

Origin: Arkina natural mineral water is harnessed at the Yverdon-les-Bains mineral bath spa, the site of important Roman mineral bath ruins. It is pumped at a depth of 726 yd in an aquiferous layer supplied by rainwater that courses for about 1,000 years among the rocky layers that filter it and give it its mineralization. After having bought the spring in 1920, a rich Armenian named it Arkina in memory of the eponymous city at the foot of Mount Ararat that was destroyed by the Turks. Poorly mineralized, Arkina is a diuretic and with its fluor content it contributes in the prevention of tooth decay. It is available in still and mildly gaseous varieties.

Composition (mg/l):		Indications:
Calcium:	37	Suitable for low-sodium diets and baby bottle preparation.
Magnesium:	22	
Sodium:	/	
Potassium:	/	**Dominant flavors:**
Sulphates:	8.8	Neutral water.
Bicarbonates:	239	**Varieties:**
Chloride:	2.9	Still and sparkling.
Nitrates:	< 0.1	
PH:	/	
Mineralization:	/	

PASSUGGER
Mineral Water (Grisons)

Origin: The first written mention of Passug water appeared in a report in 1562 on the "acidic water of Aras". In 1863, a gold prospector named Ulrich Sprecher re-discovered it while excavating in the Rabiosa gorges springs that had long been obstructed and undertook their exploitation. He sold them to Theophil von Sprecher in 1895, who founded the mineral bath spa that was well-known until World War I. After starting to bottle its water, the company experienced highs and lows until it was bought by the Feldschlosschen-Hurliman group in 1998. Passugger mineral water is rich in bicarbonates, calcium and magnesium, moderately mineralized and is gasified with carbonic gas.

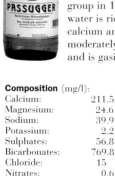

Composition (mg/l):		Indications:
Calcium:	211.5	Not suitable for low-sodium diets nor baby bottle preparation.
Magnesium:	24.6	
Sodium:	39.9	
Potassium:	2.2	**Dominant flavors:**
Sulphates:	56.8	Refreshing acidic edge.
Bicarbonates:	769.8	**Variety:**
Chloride:	15	Carbonated.
Nitrates:	0.6	
PH:	/	
Mineralization:	1,135	

RHÄZÜNSER
Mineral Water (Grisons)

Origin: The Rhazuns spring emerges from schistose rocks on the left bank of the upper Rhine in the Grisons region. Very pure, it is harnessed by a bore hole 9 yd deep. Moderately mineralized, with bicarbonates, calcium and magnesium, it contains 122.8 mg/l of sodium and its 0.8 mg/l of fluor contributes in the prevention of tooth decay. When the company that operated it went bankrupt in 1941, Passugger Heilquelle acquired the rights to the spring. In 1965, the installations were destroyed in a fire. They were rebuilt in the same location, expanded in 1975 and 1995. The spring was bought by the town council in 1996. The Feldschlosschen-Hurliman group took control of it in 1998.

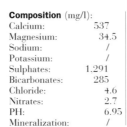

Composition (mg/l):		Indications:
Calcium:	210.2	Not suitable for sodium-free diets nor baby bottle preparation.
Magnesium:	44.1	
Sodium:	122.8	
Potassium:	5.5	**Dominant flavors:**
Sulphates:	120.4	Fresh taste.
Bicarbonates:	1,071.5	**Varieties:**
Chloride:	17.6	Still and sparkling.
Nitrates:	0.3	
PH:	/	
Mineralization:	1,643	

VALSER
Mineral Water (Grisons)

Origin: The origin of the Valser spring is thought to date back to more than 200 million years ago. At that time, a vast body of water extended from Basle to Milan, from Nice to Paris. When the continental drift brought Africa closer to Europe, the region of the primary sea was compressed for millions of years. The most varied layers of rocks, schistose, granite and limestone were each pushed on top of each other, including the region that is today the Vals Valley. The Alps were thus formed and with them, the mountain from which emerges the Vals spring, in the Grisons region. It is moderately mineralized with calcium, sodium and magnesium, with a fluor content of 0.63 mg/l that makes it useful in the prevention of tooth decay.

Composition (mg/l):		Indications:
Calcium:	436	Suitable for low-sodium diets; not suitable for baby bottle preparation.
Magnesium:	54	
Sodium:	10.7	
Potassium:	2	**Dominant flavors:**
Sulphates:	990	Freshness; small bubbles.
Bicarbonates:	386	**Varieties:**
Chloride:	2.5	Still and sparkling.
Nitrates:	< 0.1	
PH:	6.5	
Mineralization:	/	

United Kingdom

ASHBOURNE

Mineral Water (Derbyshire)

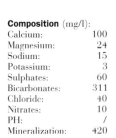

Origin: Ashbourne is a small city in Derbyshire, in an agricultural region known by tourists for its neighboring Dovedale and Manyfold valleys. The natural mineral water spring that bears its name was discovered in the twelfth century. Poorly mineralized (420 mg/l), it is low in sodium (15 mg/l) and therefore suitable for low-sodium diets and infant food. Ashbourne distinguishes itself from most other mineral waters by its "bordeaux"-type bottles. It is distributed in still and carbonated varieties.

Composition (mg/l):		Indications:
Calcium:	100	Suitable for low-sodium diets and baby bottle preparation.
Magnesium:	24	
Sodium:	15	
Potassium:	3	**Dominant flavors:**
Sulphates:	60	Neutral water.
Bicarbonates:	311	**Varieties:**
Chloride:	40	Still and carbonated.
Nitrates:	10	
PH:	/	
Mineralization:	420	

BRECON CARREG

Mineral Water (Wales)

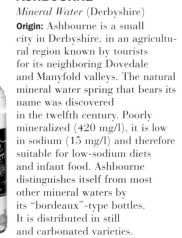

Origin: In operation since 1979, Brecon Carreg natural mineral water is one of the purest waters in Wales. Its spring is located in a protected area in the Brecon Beacons National park (386 miles² of magnificent landscapes, without industry or intensive agriculture). It is near Carreg Cennen castle, an impressive fortress built around 1300. Brecon Carreg owes its purity to its slow course through layers of basaltic and sandstone rocks before it forms an aquiferous layer 80 yd underground. Poorly mineralized (198 mg/l), it contains a large amount of calcium and mangnesium.

Composition (mg/l):		Indications:
Calcium:	47.5	Diuretic; suitable for all low-sodium diets.
Magnesium:	16.5	
Sodium:	5.7	**Dominant flavors:**
Potassium:	0.4	Neutral water.
Sulphates:	9	**Varieties:**
Bicarbonates:	206	Still and carbonated.
Chloride:	9	
Nitrates:	2.2	
PH:	/	
Mineralization:	198	

BUXTON

Mineral Water (Derbyshire)

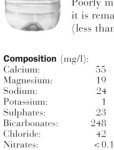

Origin: Buxton waters were enjoyed by the Romans, who called it Aquae Arnemetiae and used it to supply their thermal baths, long abandoned before being rebuilt in the sixteenth century. Between 1552 and 1567, Mary Stuart, Queen of Scotland, was (after her abdication) a regular at this mineral bath spa, whose waters were nicknamed "the jewel of mineral water springs" by the aristocracy. The Buxton spring is harnessed at a depth of 1,640 yd, in a layer preserved from pollution, one of the deepest in Europe. Poorly mineralized (280 mg/l) it is remarkably pure (less than 0.1 mg/l of nitrates).

Composition (mg/l):		Indications:
Calcium:	55	Suitable for baby bottle preparation.
Magnesium:	19	
Sodium:	24	**Dominant flavors:**
Potassium:	1	A rocky note and bitter tang.
Sulphates:	23	
Bicarbonates:	248	**Varieties:**
Chloride:	42	Still and carbonated.
Nitrates:	<0.1	
PH:	7.4	
Mineralization:	280	

CHILTERN HILLS

Mineral Water (Hertfordshire)

Origin: The Chiltern Hills spring in Alobury, Hertfordshire, was first put into operation to benefit the neighboring farms and homes. Its water began to be bottled in 1983 as a "spring water", before becoming, two years later, the first water in England to be registered as a "natural mineral water". It benefits from its location in a protected area because it emerges at the edge of the Ashridge Domain (National Trust Parkland—62 miles²). The water is filtered as it runs along the chalky rocks of the Chiltern Hills and emerges with a notable calcium content. However, it is low in sodium (9 mg/l) and suitable for low-sodium diets and the preparation of food for infants.

Composition (mg/l):		Indications:
Calcium:	101	Suitable for low-sodium diets and baby bottle preparation.
Magnesium:	2.1	
Sodium:	9	
Potassium:	1	**Dominant flavors:**
Sulphates:	4.9	Neutral water.
Bicarbonates:	299	**Variety:**
Chloride:	14	Still.
Nitrates:	6.4	
PH:	7.3	
Mineralization:	/	

COTSWOLD SPRING

Mineral Water (Gloucestershire)

Origin: Natural mineral water from the Cotswold spring was first sold in bottles in 1986 as a "spring water". It began to enjoy the official standard of "natural mineral water" in 1994. Moderately mineralized (380 mg/l) and fairly rich in calcium (133 mg/l), it is recommended for adolescents and people at risk from osteoporosis. Its poor sodium content (9 mg/l) allows it to be consumed by people restricted to a low-sodium diet.

Composition (mg/l):		Indications:
Calcium:	133	Suitable for low-sodium diets and baby bottle preparation.
Magnesium:	4	
Sodium:	9	
Potassium:	1.5	**Dominant flavors:**
Sulphates:	59	Neutral water.
Bicarbonates:	261	**Variety:**
Chloride:	22	Still.
Nitrates:	11.2	
PH:	7.8	
Mineralization:	380	

DECANTAE

Mineral Water (Wales)

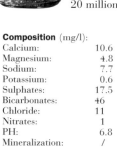

Origin: Officially recognized as a "natural mineral water" in 1986. Decantae is harnessed at an elevation of about 328 yd, at the foot of the Snowdonia mountain range in the north of Wales. It is very pure (1 mg/l), primarily thanks to the area being protected for the Trofarth Farm spring. A diuretic, its low sodium content (7.7 mg/l) allows it to be consumed by people restricted to a low-sodium diet. The producer came up with the idea of packaging a portion of his still water in sealed goblets of 86, 100 and 200 ml. This was intended for airlines and were hugely successful as he produces some 20 million annually.

Composition (mg/l):		Indications:
Calcium:	10.6	Suitable for all diets, including baby bottle preparation.
Magnesium:	4.8	
Sodium:	7.7	
Potassium:	0.6	**Dominant flavors:**
Sulphates:	17.5	Neutral water.
Bicarbonates:	46	**Varieties:**
Chloride:	11	Still and carbonated.
Nitrates:	1	
PH:	6.8	
Mineralization:	/	

FOUNTAIN HEAD
Mineral Water (Yorkshire)

Origin: Fountain Head is a very high-quality natural mineral water produced in limited quantities. Poorly mineralized (345 mg/l), its calcium and magnesium contents are notable (respectively 43.9 and 15.3 mg/l). It produces six million liters annually and is distributed in still and carbonated varieties. The spring has belonged to the Belgian Chaudfontaine group since 1998.

Composition (mg/l):		Indications:
Calcium:	43.9	Not suitable for strict
Magnesium:	15.3	sodium-free diets.
Sodium:	62.6	**Dominant flavors:**
Potassium:	5.3	Neutral water.
Sulphates:	6.4	**Varieties:**
Bicarbonates:	300	Still and carbonated.
Chloride:	60.2	
Nitrates:	< 1	
PH:	7.5	
Mineralization:	345	

GLENEAGLES
Mineral Water
(Perthshire, Scotland)

Origin: The Gleneagles natural mineral water spring is located on the magnificent estate of the same name, at the heart of Perth county, in eastern Scotland. Founded in 1985, the company that runs it, Gleneagles Spring Waters Company, located in the neighboring town of Blackford, was bought by the Time group in 1998. Poorly mineralized (235 mg/l) and low in sodium (11.6 mg/l), Gleneagles spring water is packaged in both luxurious glass bottles labelled *"Beneath the Rainbow"*, intended for big hotels and restaurants and plastic bottles, for large-scale distribution, under the name *Gleneagles"*.

Composition (mg/l):		Indications:
Calcium:	46	Suitable for low-sodium
Magnesium:	7.3	diets
Sodium:	11.6	and baby bottle preparation
Potassium:	0.7	(still water).
Sulphates:	10.7	**Dominant flavors:**
Bicarbonates:	136	Light and thirst-quenching.
Chloride:	42.7	**Varieties:**
Nitrates:	11.3	Still and carbonated.
PH:	7	
Mineralization:	235	

HIGHLAND SPRING
Mineral Water (Perthshire, Scotland)

Origin: The Highland Spring company was created in 1979 to exploit the mineral water of Orchid Hill, whose high quality has been known for centuries: John IV, the King of Scotland, granted to Blackford the privilege of brewing with this water in 1503. The rainwater (which falls on the heather-covered hillsides) runs for as long as thirty years across the red sandstone and basalt rocks which filter it and give it its mineralization before it emerges at the bottom of the hills. The site is protected from pollution, not a single agricultural project being allowed within the protected area. Highland Spring Hill is poorly mineralized, low in sodium and virtually without nitrates.

Composition (mg/l):		Indications:
Calcium:	35	Suitable for low-sodium
Magnesium:	8.5	diets and baby bottle
Sodium:	6	preparation.
Potassium:	0.6	**Dominant flavors:**
Sulphates:	6	Neutral water.
Bicarbonates:	136	**Variety:**
Chloride:	7.5	Still.
Nitrates:	< 1	
PH:	7.8	
Mineralization:	136	

PENNINE SPRING WATER
Mineral Water (Yorkshire)

Origin: A natural mineral water known in Great Britain since the beginning of the 20th century. Pennine spring water is poor in minerals (340 mg/l), with a notable content of calcium (57.6 mg/l) and magnesium (19.8 mg/l). Its nitrate content is very low (less than 1 mg/l), revealing this as a site that is effectively protected from agricultural pollution. Pennine Spring Water is distributed in still and carbonated versions. The spring has belonged to the Belgian Chaudfontaine group since 1988.

Composition (mg/l):		Indications:
Calcium:	57.6	Not suitable for strict
Magnesium:	19.8	sodium-free diets.
Sodium:	47.4	**Dominant flavors:**
Potassium:	5.1	Neutral water.
Sulphates:	16.7	**Varieties:**
Bicarbonates:	283	Still and carbonated.
Chloride:	64	
Nitrates:	< 1	
PH:	7.7	
Mineralization:	340	

STRATHMORE
Mineral Water (Tayside, Scotland)

Origin: The Strathmore natural mineral water spring is located in Forfar, in the Tayside region of the picturesque Strathmore valley. When the Scottish Parliament met in the castle of this region in 1057 to confer titles upon the nobility, the region's water was already known and enjoyed. In the 14th century, the castle was razed by King Robert I (The Bruce). Forfar and its water figures in the statistical directory of Scotland dating back to 1793. As breweries were in need of high-quality water, this site was selected for the construction of the Cameron Brewery. Strathmore water, moderately mineralized (518 mg/l), is distributed in still and carbonated versions.

Composition (mg/l):		Indications:
Calcium:	60	Not suitable for strict
Magnesium:	10	sodium-free diets.
Sodium:	40	**Dominant flavors:**
Potassium:	2.2	Neutral water.
Sulphates:	0.4	**Varieties:**
Bicarbonates:	/	Still and carbonated.
Chloride:	59	
Nitrates:	4.8	
PH:	/	
Mineralization:	518	

TY NANT
Spring Water (Wales)

Origin: Pumped in the deepest part of the Cambrian mountains, the Ty Nant spring has existed since the dawn of time but was only discovered in 1976 by a local water expert at the request of a woman named Ty Nant. Thirteen years later, the public discovered it in its exclusive blue cobalt bottle. Today, Ty Nant Spring Water's goal is to promote the brand in the global market. It is available in still and carbonated versions.

Composition (mg/l):		Indications:
Calcium:	29	Suitable for all diets.
Magnesium:	8.5	**Dominant flavors:**
Sodium:	35.8	Light and fresh.
Potassium:	1.4	**Varieties:**
Sulphates:	5	Still and carbonated.
Bicarbonates:	/	
Chloride:	12	
Nitrates:	0.1	
PH:	7.9	
Mineralization:	190	

USA

ARROWHEAD

Spring Water (California)

Origin: The Native American tribes of southern California, attracted by a curious rocky formation in the shape of an arrowhead, discovered nearby a pure spring whose high quality quickly became known. It came on the market in 1894. The water distributed today under the name Arrowhead Mountain Spring Water comes from this spring and others harnessed in the area, at an elevation of 3,543 yd, in the San Bernardino mountains. Available in still, flavored and carbonated varieties, Arrowhead water (owned by Perrier-Vittel), is distributed exclusively in California and Arizona.

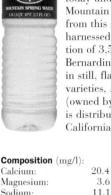

Composition (mg/l):		Indications:
Calcium:	20.4	Suitable for strict
Magnesium:	3.6	sodium-free diets.
Sodium:	11.1	**Dominant flavors:**
Potassium:	1.5	Neutral water.
Sulphates:	3.8	**Varieties:**
Bicarbonates:	81.1	Plain still, flavored still,
Chloride:	13.2	and carbonated.
Nitrates:	/	
PH:	7.9	
Mineralization:	129	

BLACK MOUNTAIN SPRING WATER

Spring Water (California)

Origin: The Black Mountain spring in northern California owes its name to the black color that the mountain at the foot of which it emerges takes on at sunset. It was discovered in 1937 by George Washington Faulstitch, who began by distributing it only within the region before turning it into a family business, which became in 1990 the biggest bottler of spring water in the United States, with a monthly production capacity of 400,000 20-liter cans and half a million cases of bottles. Poor in minerals (88 mg/l) and low in sodium, it can be consumed by people restricted to a strict sodium-free diet and can be used in the preparation of food for infants.

Composition (mg/l):		Indications:
Calcium:	7.3	Suitable for strict
Magnesium:	1.1	sodium-free diets
Sodium:	11	and baby bottle preparation.
Potassium:	1.7	**Dominant flavors:**
Sulphates:	0	Neutral water.
Bicarbonates:	45	**Variety:**
Chloride:	2.4	Still.
Nitrates:	/	
PH:	/	
Mineralization:	88	

OZARKA

Spring Water (Texas)

Origin: Ozarka natural spring water comes from the eastern part of Texas, from subterranean springs protected from pollution due to their distance from big cities and their great depth. Enjoyed since 1905, Ozarka is the most-consumed bottled water in the state. It is also distributed in the neighboring states of Oklahoma and Arkansas. Very weakly mineralized (32 mg/l), it has a very low sodium content of 2.3 mg/l and is available in still and carbonated varieties. Ozarka has belonged to Perrier-Vittel since 1987, a company that controls more than fourteen springs on American soil.

Composition (mg/l):		Indications:
Calcium:	2	Indications: Suitable for
Magnesium:	1.2	sodium-free diets and baby
Sodium:	2.3	bottle preparation
Potassium:	0.9	(still water).
Sulphates:	2.1	**Dominant flavors:**
Bicarbonates:	4.9	Neutral water.
Chloride:	3.5	**Varieties:**
Nitrates:	/	Still and carbonated.
PH:	6.5	
Mineralization:	32	

POLAND SPRING

Spring Water (Maine)

Origin: Poland Spring could be the oldest bottled spring water in the United States (documents attest to the fact that it was sold as early as 1845). 10,000 years ago, the shrinking of a glacier made room for a thick pine forest and a spring of exceptional purity. Poland Spring water is very poor in minerals (37 mg/l) with a very low sodium content (2.9 mg/l). Available in both still and carbonated varieties, it is primarily distributed in the northeast of the United States, but is nonetheless one of the two best-selling bottled waters in the country. The company has belonged to Perrier-Vittel since 1980.

Composition (mg/l):		Indications:
Calcium:	8.3	Suitable for strict
Magnesium:	0.8	sodium-free diets and baby
Sodium:	2.9	bottle preparation
Potassium:	0.5	(still water).
Sulphates:	5	**Dominant flavors:**
Bicarbonates:	20	Neutral water.
Chloride:	6.1	**Varieties:**
Nitrates:	/	Still and carbonated.
PH:	6.4	
Mineralization:	37	

TRINITY

Mineral Water (Idaho)

Origin: Trinity natural mineral water is harnessed in Paradise Creek Valley in north eastern Idaho. It emerges in an area protected by an aquiferous layer of 2.4 miles in depth, formed by water that acquires its mineralization on granite rocks that carbon 14 dating has estimated to be approximately 16,000 years old. Poorly mineralized (251 mg/l), it has a significant fluor content of 3.8 mg/l, making it useful in the prevention of tooth decay, but not recommended for very young children. Trinity is distributed in still and carbonated varieties.

Composition (mg/l):		Indications:
Calcium:	1.1	Not suitable for strict
Magnesium:	0	sodium-free diets or baby
Sodium:	55	bottle preparation.
Potassium:	1.3	**Dominant flavors:**
Sulphates:	16	Neutral water.
Bicarbonates:	69	**Varieties:**
Chloride:	8.5	Still and carbonated.
Nitrates:	<0.3	
PH:	9.6	
Mineralization:	251	

ZEPHYRHILLS

Spring Water (Florida)

Origin: Zephyrhills comes from one of the deepest springs in Florida, near Zephyrhills, "the city of pure water". It comes from an underground geological formation called Pasco High, protected from all agricultural and industry-related pollution. This aquiferous layer is fed by water that has coursed for a long time through the calcareous, sandy and silt-laden rocks that filter it and give it its weak mineralization (185 mg/l). It is available in still and carbonated varieties and belongs to Perrier-Vittel.

Composition (mg/l):		Indications:
Calcium:	58	Suitable for sodium-free
Magnesium:	3.9	diets and baby bottle
Sodium:	5.1	preparation (still water).
Potassium:	0.2	**Dominant flavors:**
Sulphates:	8	Neutral water.
Bicarbonates:	140	**Varieties:**
Chloride:	11	Still and carbonated.
Nitrates:	/	
PH:	7.7	
Mineralization:	185	

Photography credits

[40-41] Philippe Chancel/Jean-Pierre Raynaud, 1997.

[42] Forces motrices de Mauvoisin S.A.

[43] Hiroshi Sugimoto, 1987/Courtesy Sonnabend Gallery, New York.

[44] Nils-Udo, 1982.

[45] Richard Pelletier/Fotogram-Stone Images, Paris.

[46] Dugald Bremner/Fotogram-Stone Images, Paris.

[47] Michael Townsend/Fotogram-Stone Images, Paris.

[48] Amanda Clement/All rights reserved.

[49] Chris Steele-Perkins/Magnum Photos.

[50] Hulton Getty Collection /Fotogram-Stone Images, Paris.

[51] William Klein.

[52] O. Winston Link, 1982/Thomas H. Garver.

[53] Virginia Beahan and Laura McPhee, 1988/Courtesy Laurence Miller Gallery, New York.

[54] Ernst Haas/Fotogram-Stone Images, Paris.

[55] Man Ray Trust/Télimage/Adagp Paris, 2000.

[56] Pierre & Gilles.

[57] Inge Morath/Magnum Photos.

[58] The Raleigh Hotel, Miami Beach.

[59] Enrique Badulescu/Art Partner.

[60] Anette Aurell/A + C Anthology/*Elle* US.

[61] Peter Lindbergh/Light House Artist Management/*Harper's Bazaar*.

[62] TV's Bildarkiv SVT.

[63] N.D. Viollet.

[64] Prosper Assouline/Éditions Assouline.

[65] Christopher James, 1983.

[66] Bill Viola, 1996/Kira Perov.

[67] Pierre Duchier/Explorer.

[68] Picherie/Scoop/*Paris-Match*.

[69] Peter Lindbergh/Light House Artist Management.

[70] Abron/Collection SAGEP.

[71] Bernd and Hilla Becher, 1977.

[72] Centre Georges-Pompidou/Musée national d'Art moderne, Paris/ Adagp Paris, 2000.

[73] Gerster/Rapho/Robert Smithson, 1970.

[74] Carl de Keyzer/Magnum Photos.

Acknowledgments

The editor would like to thank Stéphanie Busuttil and Fabienne Rousso for their amicable and efficient contribution to the publication of this book. Thanks also to Naomi Campbell and Farida, as well as the following photographers and artists: Anette Aurell, Enrique Badulescu, Bernd & Hilla Becher, Philippe Chancel, Christo and Jeanne-Claude, Liz Collins, Lynn Davis, David Doubilet, Paul Himmel, Christopher James, Carl de Keyzer, William Klein, Peter Lindbergh, O. Winston Link, Steve Mac Curry, David Hockney, Laura Mc Phee & Virginia Beahan, Inge Morath, Bruce Nauman, Chris Steele Perkins, Kira Perov, Pierre & Gilles, Jean-Pierre Raynaud, Harald Sund, Hiroshi Sugimoto, Jean-Luc Terradillos, James Turrell, Nils-Udo, Bill Viola and Volfgang Volz.

Thanks as well to Michaël Houlette (Association des amis de Jacques-Henri Lartigue), Le Confort moderne (Poitiers), Forces motrices de Mauvoisin S.A., Thomas H. Garver, Tanya Murray (Edwynn Houk Gallery, New York), Vicki Harris (Laurence Miller Gallery, New York), The Museum of Contemporary Art (Chicago), SAGEP, Anne Druba (Schirmer/Mosel Verlag), Daniela Silberman (Sonnabend Gallery).

Thanks to the Adagp (Paris), Jennifer Bressler (Art and Commerce, New York), Candice Marks (Art Partner), Karen S. Kuhlman (The David Hockney Studio), Euro RSCG BETC / la PAC, Explorer, Sara (Michele Filomeno), Das Fotoarchiv, Marie-Hélène Kah and Vincent (Gettyone Stone, Paris), Marie-Christine Biebuyck (Magnum Photos), Maurizio Presutti (MC Photo International, Italie), Thierry Kaufman (Yannick Morisot), Photofest (New York), Petit Format, Armelle Masson and Sybille Duval (Publicis Consultants), Rapho, Roger-Viollet, Scoop, Laurence (Smile, Londres) and Télimage.

Finally, this book would not have seen the day without the precious help of the different water production companies listed in the pages of the catalog. We thank them for their contribution.